BEHIND THE WHEEL

My Life as a Cop

BEHIND THE WHEEL

by

DAN PALICKI

Fiction Publishing, Inc
5626 Travelers Way
Ft. Pierce, Florida 34982

ISBN 13: 978-0-9819727-6-3
Printed in the United States of America

First Edition

BEHIND THE WHEEL

DAN PALICKI

TOLEDO OHIO POLICE RETIRED

ABOUT THE AUTHOR

Dan Palicki retired from the Toledo Police Department (Ohio) with almost 31 years experience. He will try to relate what it was like to wear the blue uniform from early 1960's to the 1990's.

The career starts from the days in the academy, through walking a beat, filling in on various assignments getting a permanent riding crew to finishing the 31 years in the Traffic Section.

This is not a story about constant high-speed chases, gun battles, fighting someone on every call. Yes, it did happen but not like the movies or television portrays. This is only done because the public has the need for action and excitement in their lives.

This book will attempt to show what really happens – day-to-day – some good, some bad, and some comical in the every day life of a police officer. It is about the just being there day after day, constantly driving through empty parking lots and alleys, nights behind buildings checking for crime. The constant traffic duty to try and slow people down, prevent accidents and looking for impaired drivers. People do not like tickets but when you see an officer writing one, that action may well have saved you or another person on the road.

I write this book hoping that you can "put yourself Behind the Wheel" and for those who are looking at law enforcement as a career. This book may help you make that decision, as I made so many years ago. It was a good decision and there are no regrets only great memories.

I will write this in my own words and those of the people I came in contact with during those years. My partners and the public, who I truly hope were served to the best of my abilities.

During the writing of this book, Barb and I had many discussions about what being a police officer was like. Just reading or listening is one thing; you have to do the job to know the reality and to get the feel of what you experience from the boring routines and then those "adrenalin rush" times.

Law enforcement officers are the only persons that can deprive a person of their liberty and freedom – the words "you are under arrest" can change a person's life totally and completely. "You are under arrest" places a responsibility on your shoulders, as an officer, and you must know the law, be honorable, diligent, and use your most important skill "common sense". This is not a game - it is reality and actuality. This life and career is a dedication to place your life in harms way for the community you serve, to spend long and boring hours performing duties that do not make television and to be a part of a group of friends who fight the same battles and boredom.

This book is being written in two parts –the first covers the time of my new career and being with my wife, Kathy and three wonderful children. The second part started when I lost my wife and found I was now a father, alone, continuing a career and the upbringing of two sons and a daughter.

My thanks, to all who have made this book possible. My wife, Barbara, for the past 27 years, who has encouraged me to keep in focus, and for going over and correcting my many mistakes.

My thanks to all my past partners, whom I had over the many years, and whom you will meet in this book. Please remember, if you currently are in law enforcement or planning to join a department, KEEP ALL YOUR NOTEBOOKS – I did and it was the only way I could have written this account of a career from the very first day until finally the day of retirement.

PART ONE

CHAPTER ONE

Monday, April 1, 1963 9:00 AM - Oath of Office and Academy

The place is the gymnasium above the parking garage of the Toledo Police Department. I, Daniel J. Palicki, do pledge to uphold the laws and constitution of the State of Ohio and the City of Toledo.

The swearing in was done with 23 others on that day. Included in the 23 plus 4 sworn officers from other area agencies who needed to attend the academy. Sitting there during the ceremony, many thoughts cross my mind, but the biggest one was, "am I doing the right thing?" About a year before I had been talking with my brother-in-law,

Rick Ruppi, who continually talked about the fun he was having being a police officer. During the same time, my uncle, who was on the Toledo Fire Department, kept telling me what he was doing and how good a job it was.

After talking with my wife, Kathy, I decided I would take both Civil Service tests, passed both and waited to accept the one that called first. Well, here I was preparing to attend the 3-month police academy.

The basic academy staff consisted of a Uniformed Captain, plain clothes Detective/Sergeant and a uniformed Patrolman. We had guest instructors from every possible area that involved law enforcement. Each day we stood "roll call" and that would continue for the next thirty-one years for me. We maintained notebooks from the beginning and during roll call the "dope sheet" was read. The information read included stolen cars, current thefts or burglaries, any sex crimes and any new policies or procedures put out by administration. The first day the staff also dropped the bomb on us and that was to graduate you had to turn in – weekly – a typed notebook containing all the information you had learned from the various classes. That very day many wives, mothers, sisters, and girlfriends began the academy also. Remember this was way before the era of computers, it was manual or electric typewriters and not many men had ever taken that class in high school.

We were instructed in laws and ordinances, arrest procedures, rights of the arrested, firearms training, first aid including baby delivery, criminal investigation, and so much more. We were taken on field trips to the Toledo Police Jail, Lucas County Jail, Lucas County Workhouse, and Marion State Prison. Once you have visited those four locations you realize quickly that a career as a crook is not for you. A memorable trip was to an actual autopsy and then our last two weeks we were taken out and did hands-on training in “traffic control”. During class we were required to wear “good civilian” clothes and that did not include blue jeans. However, when we went out of town or the weeks we did traffic control, we had to wear suit, tie, dress shoes and a dress hat. The old days were different – picture a bunch of guys in suits and fedoras (like the old gangster movies) directing traffic – quite a sight. Nothing like today with the neat cargo pants – combat style boots – logos printed on shirts.

Towards the end of the 3 months and not knowing how to type, my typist (wife), Kathy, gives birth to our second son, Douglas. Yup, guess who had to learn a quick two-fingered version of typing – me. I came to appreciate how much work she had done with that notebook. Remember in law enforcement you have to pass everything or you do not graduate, there is no such thing as summer school or after class sessions. You make it or you are out, with no tearful goodbyes. There are others waiting to get in and you better want it or do not even try.

Again, during those last two weeks of the academy, we were assigned to attend different role calls at the department and went on a ride-along with officers to observe the routine.
The first crew I was assigned with had to do traffic control at the Jeep plant and were directing the cars in and out of the parking lot. Guess who did it? You are right me and in all the glory of the suit, tie, hat and armband telling everyone I was a “police recruit”.

Earlier it was mentioned about the friendships, well those began in the academy. Granted we were not having the high speed chases or foot pursuits; we were suffering together in long hours, long winded instructors, worry about passing written exams, and sitting on hard seats. After Friday classes, we would stop at the "Buckeye Brewery" for a couple of beers. The brewery had a taproom with a couple tables and a shelf of mason jars. Everyone grabbed a jar and had a beer. We commiserated about the boredom and planned for the graduation, being issued the uniform and getting to the fun stuff.

Of course, the best times were at the range. We were instructed in the proper use of all authorized firearms at that time. All of us had to qualify with the Smith & Wesson.38 Caliber handgun, shot gun and of course the night stick. We also were trained in the use of the various forms of tear gas.

The academy came to an end and we graduated Saturday, June 30, 1963. Where did those 3 months go? There were several things the academy gave us that were so true…

First - you will not realize how fast the time of the department will go by and how soon retirement comes. That was so true – it is almost like the blink of an eye and you really don't want it to end but the street is for the younger officers.

Second piece of wisdom imparted by the academy was "DON'T WORRY ABOUT MAKING AN ARREST, THE PEOPLE WILL, BY THEIR ACTIONS, ARREST THEMSELVES"…

LOOK OUT WORLD, HERE WE COME!!

CHAPTER TWO

JULY 1, 1963 – FIRST ROLL CALL 6:30 AM

There are two roll calls per shift for the three shifts per day and then there is a High Crime Shift, which is 8 pm to 4 am. These are your uniformed patrol shifts. In large departments, such as Toledo, had a Traffic Section, a 24 hour Records Section, City Jail, Property Room and Dispatch.

My first roll call involved standing in one or two lines with command officers facing us. Normally the Sergeant or Lieutenant would walk the line(s) for gun inspection. In those days we carried.38 Smith & Wesson's and would present them in front of us with weapon pointed down and cylinders open. This allowed the command officer to see you had a loaded weapon. He would then inspect the uniform and see that all other equipment was available such as your nightstick. As years go by - equipment changes: though in my career, I never was issued the Taser and Asp (retractable night stick), they had not been invented yet.

This first chapter will hopefully give you some insight as to terminology, which I will carry through the book. When I mention Scout or Wagon, you will know what I mean.

My very first day, I was assigned to Scout #5. At that time, all districts were two-man cars, which were called "Scout Units". Some districts were "wagons" and they were called patrols. A wagon unit was what you would term a "van" and these units would be available to haul prisoner(s) in the back. The van was equipped with u-shaped bench seats in front and on sides. These units would run a normal district and take care of calls for service, but if another unit required a back-up unit to haul a prisoner, this was their job.

The wagons were a two-man unit and when hauling a prisoner, one partner drove while the other partner sat in the back and watched the prisoner. If the prisoner became combative, even if cuffed, and attempted to create havoc, the driver would be notified or see through the window and the best way to stop the problem was a "quick stop". The one partner would see or read the other's mind, and sudden stops tend to de-fuse problems.

Back to my first call as a police officer – Scout #5 was dispatched to make a report of a strip of metal, which had come off a truck and went through the windshield of the vehicle traveling behind it. Luckily, the driver of that vehicle was not injured. The rest of the first day was spent getting advice from my partner that day. He told me about what to expect, how to handle what comes up and to know that each call will be different. People are different, circumstances are different and reactions are different.

The rest of this first month, I walked a beat in downtown Toledo. In those days, once you hit on with the box operator, you then had to hit again every hour. What was a "box"? It is a direct line phone to dispatch, mounted in a locked box on utility poles at various street intersections throughout the city. You need to remember, when I started there were no handheld "police radios". If you got in trouble and needed help, you had to look for the nearest "box" to call for back up. The invention of mobile hand-held radios was probably the greatest piece of safety equipment for a law enforcement officer. In those days, if there were quite a few of beat officers on the street at the time, a sergeant would walk with them.

The second day, July 4, 1963, I was assigned to a real treat, yah right! I was given a corner to do traffic for the Fireworks, which was held every year at Walbridge Park. The assignment lasted from 3:00 pm until the show was over. Approximately 100,000 people showed up, and, except for the usual "few people", which you will always have causing trouble, it was a great show. Those were the first two days and then I had my first two days off. At that time you would work 4 days on and 2 days off, though just out of the academy, the schedule put me at days off.

I had a good time walking the different beats. It gives you a way to meet people of the community. My normal beats were downtown when Toledo had a real downtown, with department stores, restaurants, and businesses of all kinds. This was before the concept of "malls" and everyone would go downtown to get what they needed.

When working a walking beat, you also were required to do traffic at intersections from 1:30 pm until relieved by the next shift officer. When assigned to beat patrol, you could be pulled to fill in other units for short periods of time. Officers get subpoenaed to court, and during that time, (one, two or more hours), the unit was assigned a fill in officer.

During this beginning time, I was assigned to a wagon and did drive. We were assigned to transport a lady to the hospital for an appendix attack. We put her on the portable stretcher and this was my first time to go "lights and sirens"…. WOW. When we got back into the wagon, my partner looked at me and he said, "Man, are you wet!" I looked and I was sopping wet from sweat. You will be surprised how intense the first "lights and siren" can be and how you will react.

The first month flew by and then in August, my shift was changed to afternoons – 3 pm to 11 pm. During most of my career we changed shifts every month. That month most of my assignments were filling in on various crews due to officers being on vacation. The afternoon shift is busy. Normal calls are accidents, family disturbances, missing children and a variety of any other type of report.

During the afternoon shift, I filled in on Patrol (Wagon) #4, and we were asked to transport prisoners for another unit. Upon arrival we found we had six (6) prisoners and there was no room for me to ride in the back with them. I had to ride on the outside, standing on the rear bumper and holding the overhead bar across the back door. That was a new and unique experience for the rookie.

The last day of August on afternoons, I again was assigned to Patrol #4 with Officer Bose. Bose saw a vehicle operating without lights under the bridge. We followed with out lights off also. The suspect vehicle stopped and we stopped to the rear. We both approached from different sides and turned out flashlights on at the same time to look inside. Well what did we see? Two males, one giving the other a "blow job", and truly I don't know who was more surprised – them or us. Both were arrested and we transported them to "212", which is the call number (and phone extension) for the Adult Detective Bureau. Any time a felony arrest is made, the prisoner (arrestee) is taken to the detectives to allow an more intense interview and to be sure it was a good arrest and for possible other charges to be filed. The Captain in charge was told what happened and he looked at the suspects, "asked if they wanted a stick of gum" and they were booked for Sodomy.

September 1963.

Back on days again, almost the whole month was spent walking on a beat. One day was spent at the Auto Pound. Checking in all police towed vehicles and releasing them, if allowed. It was a long day.

A special weekend was at the end of September. I was assigned with two other officers from my class to go to the Toledo Express Airport. We were there to do crowd control for the air show. I don't recall if it was the Navy's Blue Angels or the Air Force Thunderbirds. We had the best spot to watch the crowd and, of course, "the show". We even got to eat with the ground crews --- Hey, someone had to do it…

October 1962 – My first night shift. Nights were not my most favorite shift. Many officers love it however I have a problem sleeping days – too much light. Where was I, as a rookie, yup – spent most of the time walking a beat. One night was guarding two prisoners at the hospital. No problems, they were both cuffed to the bed. Tough night trying to stay awake. I was assigned a couple of nights to Scout #10 with Officer Jay Deer, who later was a Captain. We were sent to an alarm at a doctor's office. I was driving at the time and as we approached we saw two men running from the building. Officer Deer gave chase and caught his man. My man didn't run. We took them to 212 and this was my first felony arrest. They were booked for Breaking & Entering (aka B&E).

A week later, filling in one night, again with Officer Deer on Scout #10, we were watching from a hidden location and observed two men go behind the bar. After a few minutes we saw a light inside the bar, from a flashlight. They had broken in to the location. We called for a backup crew. We went to the rear and observed where they had broken in. We went inside and observed the two men taking cash from the register. This was my second felony arrest. THIS WAS VERY EXCITING AND THIS IS WHAT MAKES YOU FEEL GOOD ON THE JOB. After that I had very long night at the Board of Elections guarding the ballots. It goes from exciting/adrenalin to very boring.

Still on nights, I had no idea what was in store for me. After roll call, I was walking my beat and the Shift Captain Bray pulled up to me in his unmarked car and tells me to get in, which I do. He asked my name. He then calls into dispatch on the radio and tells them to mark me off calling any boxes for a while. As I got into the car, I said, "Yes, Sir" and he answers, "Forget the Sir crap".

We drove around a while talking. He then came to a stop behind the Gayety Theater. The Gayety was a Burlesque Theater. Captain Bray introduced me to a female who is the owner of the Gayety and a friend of his. Then they both left, leaving me standing there by myself. All the while, all the show ladies were going on the stage to do their thing. Then they returned past me in their birthday suits (that is the rookie talking – now I would say they came back by naked). As they passed by they would say, "Hi Officer". Here stands the rookie, very embarrassed, and not really knowing what to do but IT MUST BE OKAY BECAUSE THE CAPTAIN TOOK ME THERE. After a time, he came back, with a big smile on his face, and we left. He then dropped me off at my beat location and drove away. Never did totally figuring that one out.

November 1963 – Afternoons.

Most of this time was again walking a beat downtown and included the normal traffic at intersections. I finally filled in on Patrol #4 (wagon) and my partner, who was driving, pulled up to the curb at Summit & Cherry. He told me that I had to meet someone. It was a warm November and my side window was down. Up walks a very heavy lady and she comes to my side. My arm was resting on the window frame. The woman laid her breast on my arm. He (my partner) says " Meet big tit Mary"…OK, now what???

Later that month I'm filling in for a unit in East Toledo (east side of the Maumee River) on Scout #3. I am driving and I have my first accident in a police car. A vehicle was backing out of a service station driveway. I stopped and blew my horn but to no avail. He kept back up and hit the front of the police car. It was not much damage though lots of reports to be made out. It was not the first and only accident………

December 1963 – Back on days.

Again, most of the time was walking the downtown beats, with the usual traffic at intersections. A few times I did get a fixed post at Summit & Cherry and all you had there were all the drunks from all the bars. That area was the gathering place for all the sailors from the Great Lakes ships that docked then unloaded and loaded for shipment back through the lakes to other parts of our country and foreign countries. It was an active and famous place – including "Big Tit Mary". Business was good for all.

That month I did have an exciting day when working Patrol #7. We were dispatched to transport a very pregnant woman to the hospital. She was most ready to have the baby. I had to ride in the back of the wagon with her and she was getting very, very close in the contractions. She was holding my hand as tight as she could. I'm thinking, "please, please don't have the baby now!!!" We made it to the hospital on time, and I do mean just in the nick of time. No sooner did she get inside, she had the baby in the emergency room. I kept thinking what if we had not made it and she had delivered in the back with me – what would I have done – forgotten everything I learned in the academy immediately and panicked – of course. But then, it did work fine and that is how so often police work is….

The end of 1963 – my first Rookie year…what is in store for me in 1964 only the notebooks will tell.

CHAPTER THREE

1964 - START OF A NEW YEAR

January and February were spent on night shift. Whatever the shift an officer was on at the beginning of any year, it was repeated the first two months. During those months, I spent the time walking a beat (which can be very cold and miserable if you know Ohio weather), filled in on different districts. Was assigned another long night guarding a prisoner in the hospital. I was embarrassed several times by setting off alarms when checking buildings and rattling doors. But oh well, it proved I was doing my job.

Most of the time was spent on the east-side walking beat, which was both business and residential areas. At the end of the shift, around 6:00 am, two or three of us would meet at a bar called "Garvey's". They had the best and biggest Danish rolls. Of course we would have coffee or juice. It was our habit to watch the early morning activity. The bartender would set up half dozen or so drinks on the bar and men would come in, sit down, and gulp the drinks. Seconds were poured and gulped also. These were called eye-openers. The patrons would leave and head out to their morning jobs at various business, factories or refineries. All we wanted to do was get home and go to bed.

One night as I was walking through a local car dealer, I located one of the vehicles unlocked with the keys in the ignition. Remember it was winter and very cold, so to keep warm, I sat in the car, started the engine and let the heater warm up. This allowed me to observe the area for anyone on the move, who shouldn't be out. It seemed to always be there for me, or any beat officer, to use.

March finally came around and I was able to get off the hated night shift, went to afternoons, which was a little better. Throughout my career I still preferred days. With the shift change, came the change back to the walking beat downtown. During this time I made friends with a night watchman/clean-up man at one of the large department stores. Since it was still bad weather, he would let me in and we would talk a while, watch a little TV and when it was time to hit a box, he gave me the key to get back into the store. Every so often I would stop and get us burgers and bring them back to the store.

As you have figured out by now, walking beats were not filled with excitement or high-speed foot pursuits.

April brought me to days but continued me walking with the fixed post at Summit & Cherry again. I did make a few arrests for public intoxication. Several were face

down on the sidewalk with vomit all over themselves. I did work several times on Scout #11 which was the inner city. My partner was very interesting. We had a disturbance at a bar and upon entering, no one seems to have any idea why we were called. All appeared normal until we noticed a pair of legs sticking out from under the pool table. We asked who it was and again no one knew and had no idea how he happened to be under the table.
We pulled him out and his head was covered in blood. Called for an ambulance and then met them at the hospital. The man also had no idea who had injured him. This is common throughout law enforcement. He probably new but did not want to tell figuring he would take care of it himself at a later time. We completed the required reports which suspect being shown as "unknown".

In law enforcement a common call for service involves "domestics" and remember these can turn into very deadly situations. Working another district, fill-in, we were dispatched to a disturbance involved a very heated argument between the husband and wife. My partner gave them a choice – both be arrested and spend a night in jail or agree to a "police divorce". He had them put their hands on his badge and swear they would stay apart for the weekend, if not and we got called back, jail it would be. I just shook my head but he said, "it works" and it keeps them apart and us coming back.

Later filled in on a crew with an older officer and while we were at a disturbance call, a citizen told him, "I pay your wages with my taxes!" He replied, "Really! Here is about what your taxes pays for." He reached into his pocket, pulled out some change, and handed it to the man. My partner then asked him, "Are you retired?" The man answered yes and my partner then said, "Well then

I'm paying you to be retired as I am paying into social security". That shut him up.

It is now May (nights) and back walking downtown and still doing fill-ins on units. As a rookie you are assigned the least desired positions. Also as a tip, you remain a rookie until another police class is hired and on the street. It can be years before you get away from "rookie status".

Filled in on Scout #1, downtown district, and recovered my first stolen auto, had several intoxication arrests and continued to set off building alarms through my diligence to duty. May ended my first year on Toledo Police.

July brought my beloved days. Began the month walking and this included the 4th of July fireworks at Walbridge Park. No problems at all, everyone behaved and enjoyed the festivities (or didn't get caught). The next day, I was assigned a gem of an assignment. I was sent to the "middle grounds". It is an area long the Maumee River and waiting for me was my assignment. The USS Desoto County – Navy LST ship. They were there for the public to tour. While walking around and looking at the ship, one of the NCOs came to me, introduced himself and asked if I would like to come aboard. I was thrilled. He gave me a complete tour inside and out. We met the Captain who invited me to stay and observe a demonstration later in the day. I was then taken down to the mess area where we enjoyed the biggest cinnamon rolls I had ever eaten. The demonstration later involved frogmen being dropped from a helicopter, swimming underwater and setting charges to a target. They blew it up!!! Being a reader of any military book I can find, this was again a thrill of a lifetime for me.

Towards the end of the month, summer being vacation times, filled in on Scout #5 and little did I know that in the very near future, this would be my first riding assignment and having new real partners. These would be Officer Tony Novick, a 30 year veteran officer, and Officer Red Marris, who attended the academy with me. Working Scout #5, I had my first DOA. A driver lost control of his vehicle and struck a parked power equipment trailer on the side of the road. He was killed instantly. He was not intoxicated, as we had originally suspected. Since it was a fatal, the Accident Unit did the reports. As the month ended, I was assigned another gem of a fixed post.

I was at the cross walk for the Toledo Art Museum assisting patrons crossing from the parking lot on Monroe Street to the building. No one came that day; therefore I had nothing to do. To keep busy, I called the box operator and asked him a favor. He answered "Yah, what?" I asked to take a number, then times it by the next number and then times it by a third number. He asked, "What are you giving me these numbers for?"
I told him that to keep from going nuts, I had counted the number of the bricks that were used for the sidewalk, leading from the street to the front door of the museum. He hung up on me. I called him back, asking, "Why did you hang up on me?" The phone went "click" again. "Man, you just can't have any fun!"

August was nights again and again walking downtown for most of the month. Did not set off any alarms, filled in on a few crews, assigned a couple more times to the museum detail though I did not count any bricks this time. Nothing happened the entire month.

CHAPTER FOUR

September 1964 – Afternoons

My first permanent riding assignment, Scout #5, the Point Place area of Toledo with Tony and Red as partners. Still being a basic rookie, I was asking myself "What is in store for me?" The first thing any officer must do is learn the district, who belongs, what is right or not, who is acting suspicious. Keeping updated on the "house watch list" (also known in other states as a Vacation Check List). If you are gone for extended periods your local police will attempt, if time permits, to check your house while you are gone.

Our first call, with Red as my partner, was to check "for the safety" of a person that had not been heard from for a couple of days. A relative of the person was at the location to meet us. This again is a very common call for police. We knock on the door and got no response. We looked as best we could through windows around the residence. The relative gave us permission to force entry. Once inside, we located the owner, who was very sick in bed. An ambulance was called and he was transported for treatment. As usual, the incident required reports to be filed. Another note for those thinking of being a police officer, the television shows and movies seldom show officers slaving over reports. It is a part of your life and many hours are spent writing (then), though now using computers, typing lengthy accounts of the "who, what, why, where, when, and how". All reports in some form answers those questions.

Later we had a burglary at a home with a large amount of coins from a collection taken. In those cases, when it was a large amount taken, "212", the Detective Bureau was notified and a detective was sent to our scene. That month we had the usual amount of family disturbances, accidents, stolen autos, and missing children.

October we went to days and during that month, we were sent to the range as all officers must "re-qualify" with their service weapon yearly. My one partner, Tony, was one of the officers who participated in competitions with other police departments. He had won many trophies. Tony was one heck of a shot, and still is. We started out at a target which had a hole in the middle and a bell behind it. It goes "gong" when you get the round in the hole. I'm happy if I get two out of 6 but not Tony. With his revolver, waving back and forth, he gets 5 out of 6, then complains about the one he missed.

Later in the month, we found out that we were losing Tony through a transfer to another assignment. Also we all find out that we no longer will be called "scouts" and "patrols". We now will be "units" and ours will now be

Unit #6 and first roll call. To explain, most police departments work the shift process and to better utilize manpower and to allow for shift changes, they have two different roll calls per shift. This allows for half your manpower to hit-off and half still work, with the oncoming shift putting their first roll call officers out on the road, and then the second roll calls do the same. This keeps the city from being totally depleted of officers for any period of time.

During October, our daughter, Julie, is born.

November and our unit begins night. We were assigned our new partner, Joe Budkowski, and he is fresh out of a "new academy". Our class is no longer on rookie status. The first night our Shift Captain "Bray" (the one who took me to the Burlesque Theater) comes into roll call and we all burst out laughing. The Captain was wearing an oversized pair of glasses with a penis nose. He said, "This is serious business. We have a few burglars running wild on nights. You guys aren't taking your job seriously enough! I want you to go out and shake and rattle anything that is out of the ordinary. The more complaints I get from people about you that are OK. That way I know you are doing your jobs. "Now go out there and get the bastards, and dot a few eyes if you have to!" That month we had more than normal people and traffic stops. More arrests were made. In many cases people in cars have warrants, that is why traffic enforcement is so important, definitely not just making them good drivers.

Somewhere on nights, Red and I stopped a speeding car. The driver identified himself as a Detroit Police Officer and that he and his wife were just married. They had just left the reception and were trying to find a motel to spend their first night together. We looked at each other, told them to be on their way and wished them a "great honeymoon".

Our month continued with the usual driving through lots, stopping, getting out and rattling doors. We were getting a lot of complaints on our district about cars speeding on Summit Street. Summit Street is a major road, which comes into Toledo from the Michigan state line. Our north city limit is actually the Michigan state line, so there are many feeders road coming into town from there. We drove around and attempted to find a good hiding spot to catch the cars speeding into our district. Could not find one, so we drove up across the state line and found a good spot. When we spotted a vehicle traveling at a high rate of speed, we got behind them and got a "moving clock". Prior to handheld or car radar, you used your own vehicle and paced the target. Your speedometer was your radar. When they cross the line into Toledo, we stopped them and issued a citation for speeding. They would ask, "Where were you, we didn't see you?" We told them, "Hey, were the police we know where to be to catch you."

One time, while looking for speeders, a Michigan State Policeman saw us and stopped. He asked why we were up there and after explaining, he replied, "not a bad idea good hunting".

Later in the month, Joe and I were sent to do traffic at an accident on I-75 Interstate. It was snowing and the wind was blowing. The salt trucks were out and need I say more. When we were finished, we looked like snowmen. We were head to toe – snow, ice and salt. We went to Joe's house, as he lived on district, and were able to get most of the weather off us.

December we are now on afternoons. As Red and I are driving out to our district, we found a lady lying in the street. Someone had pushed her down and taken her purse. She had a broken hand. We transported her to Riverside Hospital and called "212". We told them about the purse snatching and then made our report. Later that month, with Red, we had a call about two young boy's finding a gas grenade. Confiscated the grenade, turned it over to the property room and made a report. The month continued with the usual accident reports and disturbances. On the last day of that December, New Years Eve, we took an accident report involving both drivers being intoxicated. We arrested both, transported them to the station. The breathalyzer (now known as an intoxilyzer) was given and they were booked into the city jail.

January and February 1965 – Day Shifts:

Again, on the way out to district, we were given a call to an accident. Upon arrival found one of the drivers intoxicated. We arrested him, drove to the building where he failed the breath test and booked him. As we were again heading back out to district, we were dispatched to another accident, this time with injuries. Upon arrival we found that one of the drivers was DOA. What a way to start the first day of your new year. The first accident we had to do the report, however, again with a fatality, the accident car took the report. People just forget how to drive safely when the weather gets bad.

Red and I were involved in a one-car accident while going on an emergency call. Another vehicle turned in front of us, and to avoid striking that car, Red swerved to the right going up over a curb and we hit a porch. Light damage to vehicle and porch, no injuries. The other vehicle fled the scene.

March we began afternoons. Joe and I were dispatched to see if we could get a couple of young teenage boy's safely back to shore. They had gotten on a raft that was "not theirs", untied it from the dock and the fast current in the area carried them into the Ottawa River, and from there they had traveled to Maumee Bay and into Lake Erie. It was a bad situation and they ended up very lucky. The Toledo Fire Department used a boat to rescue the boys. Once on shore they were turned over to their parents.

PALM SUNDAY 1965 is one of those memories that you wished you did not have. It is part of the job for so many but it is one of the hardest. Joe and I were listening to the crews to the west of us on the police radio. The units were reporting sighting a Tornado heading east towards us. It arrived quickly and took our car (I was driving) and moved us to the other side of the street into the curb. Oh yah, we were scared!! We then proceeded to follow the path of the tornado. It was unbelievable the amount of damage and how many homes were leveled. We assisted with rescue efforts and pulled people from under, what little was left of their homes. There were some lives lost, and many injured. All the time we were assisting victims, there were some worthless assholes that had stopped on the I-75 Interstate, climbed the fence, and were going through the belongings of the victims. We could not leave the victims and go after the looters. Victims must come first. It still, to this very day, makes me angry to think how worthless some people are in this world.

Later in the day we were assigned to keep on-lookers away from the area, and we were there until the early morning hours of Monday. The next day our unit was pulled because there were not enough officers to fill all the other districts, so much for departmental policy, we needed to be back where people could still use us.

The next day, which was my day-off, was cancelled because then President Lyndon Johnson was coming to see the damage. The remainder of that month was answering the normal and usual calls. At the end of the month we were informed that in April we were being transferred to another district. The city had just annexed a large area in the southwest of the city and they had made a new district Unit #16. So ended my time in Point Place on Unit #6. Again a note as to law enforcement, seldom do they ask you what you want to do or where you want to be – it just happens.

CHAPTER FIVE

May 1965 Day Shift:

A new district Unit #16, and little did I know that this was the start of, perhaps, the most enjoyable times on the police department. Also, with some of the best partners I ever worked with and had fun with, and are still my partners. FRIENDS TO THE END…

The newly annexed area was so large they developed two new unit, Unit #16 and Unit #15. Both units were huge areas with many open spaces and field areas. Toledo today though, you won't see the openness it is now residences, buildings, shopping malls, and complexes.

Of course, here we go again, having to learn the new district. Learning what is there and the quickest way to get to the locations. This was a totally new experience as there were no "older" officers to teach you the district.

Never takes long to find out that a large portion of calls will be accidents. Open area, open space, long roadways and people (young and old) with heavy feet. We began with a few burglary reports, several disturbances and located a few kids who were skipping school. They received a ride back to the principal's office.

One call was concerning a man who had picked up a hitchhiker. The good Samaritan then had a gun drawn on him and the hitchhiker demanded his money. The driver gave him what he had, about $60.00. The robber got mad and told him to stop the car. He robber got out and said, "Guess I'll have to try again, maybe I'll do better next time!" After talking with the victim, we called 212 and then dispatch put out a citywide broadcast with the suspect's description. End of story – wrote a report.

Just before end of the month, we were called to a house on Nebraska Avenue and the resident wanted to know if there was anything we could do about the cars speeding and squealing tires. The vehicles usually are from the White Hut Restaurant and this occurs later in the evening. The patrons are normally a younger crowd during that time. We looked over the area and told him there was no real place to set up (hide). We told him we would try our best to which he answered, "Use my driveway". His home was three doors down from White Hut. We told him we would be going on nights in a few days and would let him know when we would be there.

As soon as we sent on nights, one of our first stops was at his house and we backed into his driveway and let him know we were there. A few minutes later, two vehicles pulled out of the restaurant, lined up side by side, and took off at a high rate of speed and squealing their tires. They drag raced west on Nebraska and we took off after them, lights and siren. One of the vehicles pulled over and I got out to deal with that car. Red, who was driving, notified dispatch that I needed back up and he took off after the second car. The chase continued out into the county area and while the bad guy couldn't get away, neither could Red get to him. It was a stalemate until "bad guy ran out of gas". Red's driver was cited and arrest for multiple charges including ELUDE and the Sheriff added a few also. My driver was cited for drag racing and squealing tires, and since, he had pulled over, he was not physically arrested. There is benefit to doing the "right thing" when you are "lit up" (cop talk). Interestingly, we never went to court on either driver.

Later that month we had another chase. This driver, in his attempt to elude us, ran a stop sign, and then struck an island at the intersection of Nebraska and Holland-Sylvania Road. Heavy damage was caused to his vehicle and he suffered minor injuries. He was given first aid and then booked. We did have a few more minor traffic stops in that area but…after a while the drag racing stopped. I wonder why?? We would always pull into the man's driveway and spend time. Both he and his neighbors would give us pie, cake, coffee and pop to drink. People appreciate when you try to help them.

At the end of the month, we found out that our partner, Joe, was being transferred to another unit. Joe wanted to give Red something to remember him and got me in on the plan. So ----- imagine this ----two uniformed officers, around three in the morning, chasing a duck at Sleepy Hollow Pond, trying to catch it and all the while this duck is quacking loudly. Finally we did capture it and put it in the back seat of the patrol car. We continued to listen to the quacking and praying we would not get a call (or having to clean up anything in the back seat). We made it to Red's apartment. He lived on the next district, so we weren't too far out of ours.

Joe grabbed the duck, walked up to Red's door (knowing he never locked it) and put the duck inside – all the while; this duck is quacking and continued to quack. We sat out front and suddenly the front door opened and there stands Red holding the duck, yelling "What the fuck am I going to do with this duck?" Joe yells at him, "I wanted to give you something to remember me by. So long partner! We drove away. It was heart-warming – the things you do to friends that you would work with and would die with in a heartbeat.

The next night I worked with Red and asked him what he did with the duck. He said he put it in the swimming pool at the apartment complex and it quacked the rest of the night. It was so long to another partner, though we did have a great time though it was so short.

CHAPTER SIX

AFTERNOONS

We are assigned our new partner, Officer Bill Adama. What will he be like? Will we all get along? Better yet, will he like us?

Bill and I worked our first day and started it off with an accident. One of the drivers was intoxicated. We took him to the building, administered the "test", he failed and was booked.

During this month and as usual on days and afternoons, we get many summons and subpoenas to serve. Every so often, we have a warrant or two. Working days, you get a lot of church traffic and on occasions do traffic duty to get them in or out of the church lots.

We made many new friends and were invited to a lot of meals, while working. We did go to a few picnics. We also made friends with the firefighters at Number 14's Engine House on Reynolds Road. As like us, they also were new to the area. We would spend a lot of time with them, having lunches and dinners. Many times they would call us at home to find out if we wanted to eat with them once we came on shift. Trust me, we had many excellent meals – firefighters are good cooks. Nothing of great excitement happened the first couple months – the usual accidents, domestics, few injuries and lots of reports.

We began having some problems with the juveniles in our district. We needed some way to keep track of them, so we went to Rogers High School on our district. We asked them for a current yearbook. After telling them why we wanted it, we were provided one. Whenever we had a contact with a juvenile, we cut out the picture, glued it to an index card and added DOB, contact information, any vehicle information. We called it our "281" file. Any contacts were noted on the card. "281" was the record bureau extension; it was now our on-street record section. It was a great help to us.

One thing we noticed quickly was each shift had its own set of people and each shift was totally different. You could meet them on days or afternoons and they acted the same but when you had contact with them on the night shift, they would for some reason be weird acting. There is a saying, "when there is a full moon people change" – it is true.

DAYS:

This month we spent much of the time serving summons and warrants. We had some very bad and fatal accidents on this shift. A fatal occurred while Bill and I were working. This accident involved a large panel truck that pulled out from South St. to go left on Reynolds Road. The driver of the car was on Reynolds and was struck by the panel truck. We were first at the scene and got the driver out of the car. As Bill was trying to help the driver, he died in Bill's arms. He was in his early teens. Those are one of the tough ones.

Another accident was when Red and I were partners. This one occurred on Reynolds at Hill. A vehicle with two people was making a left turn to go west on Hill Ave. A fully loaded cement truck struck the car to the right side. The impact killed the passenger and the driver was partially thrown from the car. The impact was so severe that both sides of the vehicle were almost touching. The driver was killed when the car was pushed over on the road. Both accidents involved left turns in front of on-coming vehicles.

One morning Bill and I were looking for a stolen vehicle in a wood area off Dorr St. We did find it however the poison ivy found me. I was off work for a couple days.

Bill and I were sent on a call to see some very irate neighbors. It would seem that a neighbor of these people had been playing hot rod with his car on the streets. They had ask him to stop and he laughed at them, giving them the finger and took off at a high rate of speed. We located the driver from the description they gave and we talked to him. He said that he did not do what they said. He returned to the neighborhood and did the same thing and told the residents that the "cops can't do anything to me because they can't see me do anything and can't catch me!!"

We were dispatched back to the scene and we told them what the plan was but it would require them all to be willing to testify in court. If we didn't see someone do it, we had to have witnesses and the more the better. The neighbors were told that the moment he drove out to call dispatch and have them immediately radio us to call "290", which was our cue that he was on the road. Dispatch was told of the plan and agreed. We intentionally drove by the suspect's residence as we left. A short time later we get the "290" call and while we did not see him drive; we went to his house and cited him. It was found with a driver's status from before that he was suspended, so with the citizens' help and testimony, we cited him. He did go back to the area but had someone else drive and told the neighbors the cops gave me a ticket. I'll see you all in court and go fuck yourselves. We all did go to court and after the judge heard everyone, he was found guilty, had a stay in jail and paid a hefty fine along with the judge recommending that he move from the area.
A lesson to learn, don't push the envelope, we may not win the first time but we are far better at the game and what goes around will come back around.

As I had previously mentioned, due to the vastness of the area, driving complaints were many, we now had a problem of drag racing in the Angola Road area. The residents reported that someone had painted a white stripe across the road and then 1/4 mile further down was another white stripe across the road. We told them when we got back on nights we would see about putting a stop to the racing. We just had to wait for the right time with this problem.

We had one bar on our district called "Lavoy's" and all the locals usually went there on days however they had a younger group, including Toledo University students, at night. One morning Red and I were sent there on a disturbance. We asked the bartender what the problem was and he told us he had taken care of it. We ask what and he said that some guy couldn't wait to be served, so he came around the bar and started helping himself. I told him to get back and he refused. The bartender stated he pickup a bar stool and struck the man with it. We asked where is the man now? The bartender said Oh; he's still behind the bar. We looked and there he was totally awake, sitting on the floor with a bloody head. We called an ambulance that took the injured man to the hospital. Before leaving we asked him if he wanted to prosecute and he said no. Made out the appropriate report and that ended days.

MIDNIGHTS:

There were many nights that we did not get any calls. Talk about long and boring. We would attempt to keep active with many building checks, driving in and out of driveways, vacation checks, watching bars at closing for possible drunk drivers or fights in the lots.

One night on our way out to district, Bill and I were dispatched to a silent alarm at the National Bank at Dorr & Reynolds. We looked at each other with big question marks – how do you get a silent hold up alarm at night? We checked around the building and came to the drive thru window. Someone had taken a cement block and smashed out a window. Though very thick, they had managed to get in. Once inside the suspect had taken all the dollar bills that were in the drawer at the teller's area. The bills that he grabbed were the ones that the teller "gives to the robber" which set off the alarm and start the cameras filming. The window didn't set the alarm and if he had grabbed any other money, he might have gotten away with it. Never did find out if they got him but they did get pictures. The usual reports and detective notifications made.

During this time my partner and I ran across a young man for speeding. We will call him Jim and something told us that this would not be the only contact, so we added him to the 281 file.

One night we had a disturbance with a family on Nebraska Avenue, little did we know we would be spending a lot of time with them. In fact we were there so much, we were all on a first name basis. Midnights continued and we had several disturbances at "LaVoys". In those situations, we would give the involved persons a choice – either call a cab or ride with us to jail. On one of these calls, we went inside, resolved the issues and left a calm bar. At the end of the shift, we did the usual car clean up and found a six-pack of beer in the back seat. We later learned that the bartender and it was his way to say thanks for just doing our job. This was not the only call there or the only surprise package in the back.

Remember the white paint stripes for drag racers, well Red and I were parked on Angola Road and observed six cars lined up, two at a time, waiting to take turns. The first two took off at a high rate of speed with tires squealing. This was our cue, and we did the same with the red lights on. We sped past the four remaining cars in line and they miraculously disappeared. We caught the other two and the looks on their faces were "priceless". Each driver was cited for Drag Racing and Squealing Tires. At that time, the traffic offenses did not "require a trip to court" they just had to pay the fines.

A few more captures and the drivers moved their location. They realized that painting their own starting lines and finish lines was not real smart. They also thought that by going to another area and just using landmarks for the race would get them home free. They thought that by starting in the city and then crossing the line would get them out of tickets. Did not work and finally they just tired of the game.

One night, still December 1965, and the roads were ice and snow. Officer Adama and I were following a suspicious car that was south on Reynolds Road and when we reached Dorr Street, the road curves to the right. During the turn, our car slid to the left and struck a raised cement island. I am not sure to this day what happened next. I woke up in the hospital.

It seemed that Bill, who was driving, was thrown out of the driver's side door. I was thrown out the driver's side door also and struck my head on the doorframe. And that is what you get for not wearing "seat belts". Though it was not common practice in those older days for police to wear seat belts. It was "what if you have to jump from the car to foot chase a bad guy", takes too much time. No, not true and I began wearing my belt no matter what and still do. We both spent five days in the hospital. One night Bill and I were playing cards with another patient and the nurse came in and raised hell with us. It seemed the man was to have brain surgery the next morning and was to have total quiet and no activity. It was a rousing game and if we had been quieter, we would not have been caught. Both Bill and I were off a total of twenty-three days. Lets go back to work!!!!

We were back on nights and Bill and I were stopped at a red light on Reynolds at Dorr St. Our light changed to green and immediately a vehicle on Dorr Street ran the red light right in front of us. We started after him and he refused to stop. He sped up and was heading for the city limit. We continued the pursuit and notified dispatch we had left the city. The county was contacted for assistance.

I pulled up next to the vehicle and the driver looked over at us. He then swerved his vehicle left into us and struck our right side. We got back behind the car and stayed with him. We could see a car with red lights on coming towards us. It was a Sheriff's car sent to assist and he headed straight towards the suspect car forcing it into a ditch. Before they could get out and run, we got to the vehicle and pulled driver and passenger out. Both were intoxicated which was obvious from the smell and actions of both. The Sheriff's deputy arrested the driver for DUII and the passenger for just being drunk. We also cited the driver for various things especially his "ramming" of our car.

Another interesting call for Bill and I involved the fact that Bill had been partying before coming to work that night. I would not let him drive. In those days you always took care of your partners. We were patrolling at the farthest end of our district and received a call of a possible DOA. A female resident had gone to bed and her husband stayed up to watch television. She woke up and he was not in bed with her. She got up and found him slumped in his chair. She could not get a response and call the police. When we arrived, Bill popped the trunk and got out our first aid kit. The man was cool to the touch. Bill started giving him mouth-to-mouth resuscitation. The wife said, "that is a very strong first aid kit you have, I can smell the medications that you are using." I said, "yes, we just refilled it when we started work tonight". Did you figure it out? She smelled Bill's breath from the earlier party before work. The gentleman had been dead for quite a while but you always try, if just for the family. 212 was notified and we stayed with his wife until a relative could arrive and arrangements were made for transport. The death was not in any way suspicious and 212 did not send a detective. We handled the call and reports.

On nights, there was a very popular restaurant in the area, the Secor Grill. Everyone went there including the police. It was located at Dorr and Secor and was always busy. You almost needed a reservation to get served. With it being popular with the police there was a minimum of one car there during business hours, which was 24x7. At night partiers from the bars would go there for coffee and food, though there were never any fights or trouble. Secor Grill had great food all times of day and night.

AFTERNOONS:

We were now back to accidents, serving subpoenas, and a warrant or two. One afternoon, Bill and I were sent to a big family disturbance on Hill Avenue near the city limits. When we arrived at the house, a male answered the door and said, "Oh, you're new here. This is my house and I can do what I want, and you can't arrest me!" Bill and I looked at each other, knowing and thinking, "guess who's going to jail!" You never tell any police officer "you can't arrest me", especially because you are in your own house. Those few words get you in more trouble than necessary. Yes he did go to jail for intoxication and disturbing the peace.

Some time later, we were dispatched back to the same address on a disturbance. The same man answered the door, looked at us and said, "Oh it's you guys, it's not me it's my wife". We ended up arresting the wife, as she was highly intoxicated and attempting to fight her husband. We called a wagon to transport her.

Later that month, it was just starting to get dark and Bill and I were taking a short break. We were just off Hill Ave. in a field, looking across Hill towards Nebraska Ave. We observed two motorcycles coming off Nebraska on to McTigue St. They lined up and off they went at a high rate of speed heading towards us. Bill was driving and started out towards with red lights on. One cycle passed us with the other one turning left off McTigue on to school property. He turned his head light off and headed towards the football and baseball fields. We followed him and watched as he ran into a fence which was about three feet high. Needless to say the cycle stopped suddenly but he didn't. He was wearing white pants and we could see the white airborne over the fence and then the pants got up and starting fleeing on foot. Apparently he wasn't injured, but guess what – remember our mentioning a Jim. We ran the plate on the motorcycle and guess who owned it? Using our little 281 file, we had all his contact information. We waited for a tow to get the motorcycle and then drove over to Jim's, rang the bell and when the parents answered we handed them all the various citations we had written. We told them "Jim knows what this is about". Interestingly, we never went to court on those citations.

Remember the accident that Bill and I had, well about the same time another crew had a similar accident. Both vehicles were basically totaled. What did the city do, well they cut both cars in half and put the two good ends together and made one. YES, we got assigned the car. It actually held up until later in the year when they actually got new cars in.

On April 28, 1967 our new and very good partner, Bill, was transferred to another crew. To this day we are still good friends. He is still my partner!!!!!!!!!!! We had lots of good times and fun doing it.

CHAPTER SEVEN

MAY 1967 NIGHTS

We have another new partner, Officer Bob Bannon, and the same question – will we get along? He started the month with Red and I did not work with him until the 3rd of May. For some reason we had a lot of accident reports. Most were little or no injuries, however, we did get one fatal. Red and I were working together. It took place about a half mile north of Dorr St. on Reynolds Rd. We were not the first unit on scene. Our fire fighter friends from #14 engine house arrived first.

The accident happened within a few hundred yards from the firehouse. It was a single vehicle accident. What appeared to have happened was the driver took off at a high rate of speed north on Reynolds from Dorr. He came to the curve in the road and lost control. The vehicle went left of center across two lanes of southbound traffic, up over the curve, where he struck a large steel utility pole. The impact was to the right side of the vehicle and was so severe the passenger in the right front seat was trapped. He was trapped between the pole and his seat, which was pushed into the back seat.

The only way to get the passenger out was to use two tow trucks. One pulled from the front and one pulled from the rear. We could hear the passenger calling to us – "Help, don't let me die". There was not much we could do for him at the time as no one could get to him and no medical aid was possible. He had serious injuries and his intestines were literally exposed. Once he was removed, aid was given and he was transported however he did not survive his injuries. The driver was seriously injured also but not fatally. The impact was so great that the motor was torn from the frame of the car and was laying approximately 50 to 60 feet north of the point of impact. Again, so often the driver is at fault for drinking, speed or both and they live through it and passengers die.

On another night, Red and I just happened to turn onto Angola Rd., west off Reynolds, and we saw two vehicles take off at a high rate of speed. They were side-by-side, tires squealing and we had another drag race in progress. We gave chase. At the intersection of Angola at Holland-Sylvania, one made a left turn and the other went straight. We chose wrong, we went after the vehicle that went out of the city. It was one of the fastest cars we had ever seen. We never did catch him. You can't get them all!!

Another night we were back at LaVoy's Bar on a disturbance. When we arrived we saw several customers outside drinking. They were told to go inside to drink. One of them looked at us - drank the beer and then let the bottle drop from his hand. Before it hit the ground, we had him inside the police car and under arrest. The charges were intoxication and littering. Due to his condition we called for a wagon to transport.

BACK ON AFTERNOONS:

By now you should be well aware of how each shift has its specific routines – accidents, subpoenas, summonses, and warrants. The reason for the warrants being more active is the potential for finding people at home for supper or early evening. This is also the reason for family disturbances. They are home and together. We now had the chance to introduce our new partner Bob to the "friends" we had made since coming to this district.

Red and I ran across our friend, "Jim", driving a car. Remember Jim and his flying off the motorcycle at the school. When checking him during that incident we had found that his driver's license was suspended. Needless to say, we pulled him over. He was cited and arrested. A wagon was called for transport and a tow was called for the vehicle. He apparently doesn't learn quickly. As in many incidents, the vehicle he was driving was not his and the owner would be paying the tow and storage charges. One lesson you try to get out to the public is that you don't loan your car to anyone – do you really know they have a valid license?

Cars just seem to bring out the worst and stupidity in people. Red and I observed a vehicle pull out of the White Hut restaurant with a man lying on the hood with his arms and legs spread out. He was on his belly facing forward and it looked like he was flying. Again this was a given – we pulled them over. Surprisingly the guy on the hood was not drunk as we had assumed. The driver was not intoxicated either. They were both cited for "Clinging to a Motor Vehicle" and the driver was issued a "Due Regard for Safety".

We did not go to court on the driver but we did appear on the "flying man". When the judge heard what we had occurred, he asked the defendant, "Did you enjoy what you did?" He replied with a smile, yes! The judge replied, "I hope you also enjoy the $50.00 fine.

DAYS:

Days were as usual, lots of reports, and of course, Sunday church traffic. July 1967 brought the city's first period of CIVIL DISTRUBANCES AND RIOTS. They began towards the end of the month and the entire police department began workings 12-hour shifts with <u>3-Men Crews</u>. Two to three officers would work together on the walking beats. The primary problems were in the Dorr and Detroit area. These began as a spill over from the civil problems in Detroit, Michigan. The riots were occurring in many other cities throughout the country and Toledo was not left out. The initial reason for the unrest was equal rights for minorities. This was not going to end with just one riot. Also while the need for equal rights was valid, so many others use the atmosphere of unrest to commit crime or just enjoy causing damage and or injury.

Listening to the dispatchers sending our crews to the various calls in that area was interesting. It was an eye opening experience. The calls varied from checking on people acting suspiciously, fighting, breaking store windows and looting, to a person walking with a "six-pack" of Molotov cocktails (fire bombs). Thankfully during this period of unrest, there were no serious injuries either to police or the public. There were a number of arrests made involving drinking, fighting, thefts, loitering and the usual outstanding warrants.

I do not blame those involved for wanting to get a better life but I do not and will not ever accept the smashing, breaking and destroying anything to reach a goal. Also looting and theft is just as it states – there is no logical reason except greed and preying upon those who are not involved. It was no different than the low life's that looted during the tornado.

The end of August, we again were faced with training a new partner. Red put in for a position in the Traffic Bureau and was accepted. Goodbye Red, we had a lot of good times for the past three years. Good luck on your new job.

CHAPTER EIGHT

AFTERNOONS 1967

Our new partner is Officer Doug Baden. Doug and Bob graduated from the same Police Academy class over one year before. Our crew now consists of Bob, Doug and me. Little did we know that we three would remain a crew for five years, and what was in store for us?

An interesting situation happened when Doug joined us. The City purchased new cars "Matadors" and they came with Air Conditioning (wow a new fangled gadget) "but" they had them all disconnected. The city decided that since the wagon crews did not have air conditioning then it would not be fair for the street crews to have it also. So again – all summer (Ohio – hot – humid) we all sweat our Asses off. We even tried to block off the vents to keep the hot air from blowing in – didn't work. A year later we all did get air conditioning.

We had five of our days off cancelled during the next few years for what they called "In Service Training". At some of the sessions we had "riot training". Apparently the system learned from the prior civil period that we needed updating. We were shown and performed all the various formations that are used during a riot. You must move large groups and attempt to disperse them. The training was interesting in the dynamics of large group control. Part of the system is to make sure the crowd does have openings to disperse, you do not want to "corner them" without an escape route. The outcome you want is breaking the situation apart and stopping the violence. Most rioters have common sense kick in and they just want to leave. The violent fighters won't and those are the ones you only want to deal with.

We were given new riot helmets and we were to use them daily. The helmets replaced the uniform hats and we had them for approximately three years.

In 1968 we were having problems with the city during wage negotiations. The city stated they did not have any money to give us a raise. The city stated, "if you want a raise, go ask the citizens of Toledo." Well, we along with the city fire fighters did just that. We had all our people out with petitions getting signatures to have our raises put on the ballot at the next general election. We were at shopping centers, intersections; door-to-door in neighborhoods and anywhere else we could find people to sign the petitions. The backing we got from the residents was tremendous.

Once the city saw what we were doing and how well it was received and they saw the "light". The city asked, "if we support the levy can we add a small percentage to help the city?" The tax was an actual city income tax, not property tax. Any one who worked within the City of Toledo would pay an income tax of.50% (half a percent) with l/4 going to the police/fire and l/4 going to the city. It was readily passed because the citizens knew very well that your police and fire are your front line and work for them.

In 1969 I was offered a chance to work a great "project". Project is a term used when you are allowed to work certain jobs "off duty". Projects gave officers a chance to earn extra cash. The chance I was given was at the University of Toledo. We were there to assist the University Police with traffic control at all the parking lots during games and special events. We also did security inside for the same games and events. Once we got all the cars in, we would then go inside and enjoyed watching the games or special entertainers who were appearing. Just before the program or game ended, we would then report back to our assigned positions and get everyone out of the lots.

I worked part-time for the TU for 25 years, until my retirement. I always used the money to save and pay for vacations and trips to the west. Plus the savings helped with our ultimate move, when we retired, to the State of Oregon.

During my projecting at TU, I worked almost half the time with Officer Gary Cooke. Over time we became good friends and still to this day remain friends with he and his wife. During the many years we would end up taking the 3-4 day trips to Las Vegas as a group – Gary, Bob and our wives. During 1969 we, my wife Kathy and I, took our first trip out west. We visited some friends who had moved to Seattle, WA. On the trip, I fell in love with the WEST!!!! I immediately knew that I would be in the west after I retired.

Almost every year after that, I planned vacations out west. We drove through every state and I continued to watch for that "special area" that would be the retirement home. After years of looking, Oregon was the place.

In 1970 I was issued my original badge – number "432". It was replaced a period of time later with 242. Periodically badge numbers changed as people leave through whatever reasons. It can be through retirements, quitting or, sadly, death. The badge number was a mark of seniority.

During 1970, the police department was offered the chance to purchase from the US Government surplus.30 Caliber M-1 Carbines. They were offered at $40.00 plus an extra $10.00 each to cover the cost of sending some officers to pick them up. My carbine was stamped as being made in 1944 and was still in original packing grease. It remains in pristine condition today. If you only knew then, what you know now – I would have purchased several more. At that time though and with a family, $40.00 was still a lot of money. I always tried to think of my family first and "man toys" was not in our budget.

1970 brought to Toledo a terrible incident when one of our fellow officers was murdered. While he was sitting in the patrol wagon, and his partner had gone into a restaurant to get them dinners, a "coward" walked up and shot him. He died instantly. His partner came out and saw what happened and went hysterical and into shock. The partner was his good friend and black. They were what were known as a "salt and pepper" crew. It took a long period of help and support before the partner could return to work. He was immediately taken off the street and given an inside job. The shooting took place at Dorr and Detroit area. This was during the period of time when different groups throughout the country were saying, painting on walls and in newspapers to "Kill the Pigs", of course we being the pigs.

The department raided the local "Black Panthers" head quarters which was a few blocks from where the officer was murdered. An arrest was made, however, after a long trial, the subject was set free due to a hung jury.

The fallen officer had a very impressive funeral, which hopefully would never be seen again. The afternoon before the funeral, Doug and I were pulled from our crew to stand as Honor Guard at the funeral home during visiting hours. The day of the funeral officers from all over the State and Country attended. Everyone marched in the street from the funeral home to the church and then to the cemetery. Luckily we did not lose any more officers during my time on the police department. One is too many.

In 1972 our police union was changed from the PBA (Patrolman's Benevolent Association) to the TPPA (Toledo Police Patrolman's Association). The TPPA replaced the PBA and the FOP (Fraternal Order of Police) as the Police Bargaining Unit. We are still members of both the FOP and TPPA Retirees units.

Also during this time the police were catching a "lot of Hell" while the Vietnam War was going on and other civil disturbances throughout the country. We became expert in having all kinds of objects being thrown at us and continuing to be called "pigs". It is difficult to maintain self-control during those times. When we were being called pigs we would tell them “thanks” then explain to them, if they would listen:

DO YOU UNDERSTAND THAT “PIGS” ARE ONE OF THE MOST INTELLIGENT OF ANIMALS? AND “PIG” STANDS FOR

P…PRIDE
I…INTEGRITY
G…GUTS”

CHAPTER NINE

DAYS

Ah.............Yes, the good ole days. Summons, warrants, traffic and since it is winter, lots of accidents. Why is it that when any bad weather strikes, people forget how to drive even though it happens yearly and nothing is new? We mostly had non or minor injuries during that time.

One morning, Doug and I took a burglary report. It happened at an insurance company located at Dorr and Secor. Entry was made through the rear door and after taking several items, the suspect left a note saying "Sorry, I left the door unlocked" and signed it with an "X". 212 notified and a detective was sent to the location for follow-up.

We had a few missing children reports and luckily they were all found unharmed. Most had just wondered off and some were not happy with parents after being punished. Located a few students who were skipping school and we provided a ride back to the principal's office. They just were not happy with the service we provided.

Another morning, Doug and I were sent to a local bank as someone had called to tell them "there is a bomb inside your vault and I will set it off unless you give me $200.00". The caller had then hung up. We all thought that $200 was an odd amount to ask for and not telling the bank "how to deliver the money"!!!! Criminals can be so stupid. We stood by at the bank until a detective arrived for follow-up – whatever that could be – well unless the "great bank robber" called back and said where he was……….

One Sunday morning, Bob and I were dispatched to a disturbance on Nebraska Ave., our old friend's home where we had been many times before. As we pulled up, we observed one of the daughters hanging onto the outside mirror of a moving vehicle, screaming, "Don't leave me. I love you." The car stopped when the driver saw us. Once things were calmed down, the driver said that he was, but not anymore, her "boyfriend". He continued stating that they (her family) were NUTS!. He had enough with them and was leaving. As he left, the girl continued to yell and cry, "I LOVE YOU". It was one of those calls that you had to be there, see it and still not believe it.

Late one morning Doug and I observed a vehicle at the side of the road, facing the wrong way, on Hill Ave. We stopped, got out and approached the car. We observed two men inside fighting. One of them had a GUN. We drew our weapons, yelled for them to stop and throw out the gun". We then ordered each to exit – one at a time – and we handcuffed them. We picked up the gun and it was loaded.

We determined who the owner of the car was and he had seen a guy hitch hiking on Hill out in the county. He stopped and picked him up. After a period of time the hitchhiker pulled the gun and demanded money. He drove for a while and he finally caught the guy off guard and they started fighting over the gun. This was just before we arrived. We called for a wagon for the suspect and had the vehicle towed for evidence. We transported the victim to 212 for statements. The suspect was subsequently booked for Armed Robbery.

Another morning Bob and I were sent to an apartment complex on Dorr at Byrne. The complex had a recreation area for residence and this morning the manager had found a young teen playing basketball. He asked him to leave which he did as the teen did not live in the complex. A short time later he again spotted the teen playing basketball. When he told the boy to leave, the boy picked up a rock and threw it at the manager. He missed him but ended up hitting a sliding glass door to one of the apartment. The boy ran towards the railroad tracks that ran behind the complex. The manager gave chase, caught the teen, brought him back and called us.

We noticed the teen had a bloody nose and asked what happened? He said that he fell on the tracks when he chased me. We called "257" (being the juvenile bureau) and explained what had happened. We also told them we had tried to contact the teen's parents but got no response by phone. It was always policy to notify a parent when a child was involved in a crime. We took him to 257 where he was charged with Criminal Damage to Property. On our way back to district, dispatch contacted us and instructed us to return to the apartment complex for further information.

When we got there, the manager asked us what the boy had said about his bloody nose? We told him nothing. The manager then told us that when he caught the boy, the boy had told him “I know my rights”. The manager said, so he gave him his rights, a right fist in the nose. He then told him that if he told the police that he hit him, he would find out where he lived and hurt him. We advised him that he should contact us should anything further happen and we never received a call.

Another morning Doug and I get a call of an Attempted Break-In – suspect gone. We were given a suspect description – black male, light colored clothing, driving a green 4- door car, make unknown, Michigan plates and the suspect would have a cut on right hand.

Upon arrival at victim’s residence, an older lady met us at the door and we asked her what happened. She replied that she was looking out her front window. She watched a black man get out of his parked car, walk up and down the street about a half a block each way. He then walked up to her front door and rang the doorbell. She said she did not answer and he then left the front door. He walked around the side of the house and then knocked on the back door. She said she did not answer it and then he tried to open the door but it was locked. He then picked up something and knocked out a small windowpane in the door. He was reaching through to unlock thc door and she said she grabbed a knife and stabbed his hand, He screamed and ran to the front, got in his car and drove off very fast. She said she then called for us. We asked her, how long was it before we got to her home after she called. She said about six or seven minutes. We put out a general broadcast on him and the car, also an alert to the hospitals for them to watch for cut hands. She told us that after he (the suspect) had left she cleaned up the mess, blood, glass and knife. Either she was very lucky and brave or very foolish for not having called the police sooner.

CHAPTER TEN

AFTERNOONS

Afternoons began with the usual however there seemed to be an increase in armed robberies especially at gas stations. We were back with the great meals at Engine House #14.

On April 5, 1968, a horrible day for all America, Martin Luther King was shot and killed. The entire police department was called in early to work. I worked a 17 1/2 hour day. The department wanted to have enough officers on duty in case of possible riots and other types of disturbances. Though grieving, the citizens of Toledo were orderly and nothing happened.

One afternoon, Doug and I were dispatched to a suicide. My first! A woman had shot herself with a.38 revolver in the head. Her husband said she had gone outside the home and he heard a shot. He went out back and found her lying on the ground. He saw a gun on the ground next to her. He went inside and called the police. He went back outside; picked up the revolver, put it back inside the house. Stated he put it back in the closet where she had found it. We asked him, "Why did you take the gun into the house?" He could not give us an answer. We thought it might have been a response caused by the shock of the suicide. We went and retrieved the gun for evidence. The husband told us that his wife had been under the care of a doctor for a couple of months and was taking numerous medications.

While making out our report, a detective was sent by 212 to the scene. The coroner also arrived. We notified family members to come to be with the lady's husband in order to help him cope with the situation.

Another afternoon, Bob and I were sent to a jewelry store where they were attempting to hold a suspect who had stolen a check. The check was worth $600.00. As we walked into the store, the suspect somehow got the check from the store manager and ATE it. He refused to tell us how he got the check. 212 had us transport the suspect for questioning and the manager was asked to follow us in to the building. We never did find out the "end of the story".

One summer afternoon Bob and I were sent to an apartment building on Hill Ave. and met by the manager. He reported that some people living there told him there was a strange odor coming from one of the apartments on the second floor. Stated he knocked on the door and no one answered, so he called us. We approached the door and noticed a definite aroma coming from the apartment. We knocked and received no response. We called out the resident's name and again no response. We told the manager to use his master key and open the door. He was then told to wait outside.

We entered the apartment and wow, what an aroma. In the kitchen we found a lady lying on the floor. There was a small pool of dried blood by her head. We observed a cut in her scalp. We examined her body and she was deceased. Looked around the kitchen, we saw a step stool was lying on its side next to the body. We also saw that a door to a wall cabinet was open. Apparently she was on the step stool, attempting to get something from the cabinet and somehow fell. She struck the side of her head on the corner edge of the counter, which appeared to be cause of death.

My partner in an attempt to cover the horrible smell got a cigar from someone and started to smoke it. Needless to say it did not help that much even with the windows open. A detective was dispatched along with the coroner. The detective asked the manager a few questions and was getting ready to leave. We asked him "aren't you going inside to see the body?" You could see that he really did not want to go in because of the smell. He finally took a piece of cloth, put it over his nose, ran in and in one motion was back out. As he left he said, "She's dead". After the coroner left, the body was taken to a local mortuary, as we were unable to locate any family members to make decisions.

Doug and I were sent on a "Man Shot" call. Upon arrival at location we found two intoxicated males inside. We noticed that one of them had some blood on the side of his head. We then saw a lot of holes on one of the walls. We checked him further and the bullet had entered and followed the scalp around and exited out the back of his head.

We asked what happened and they said they were drinking and telling each other who was the best shot. They decided to find out! What they did was, while one of them sat in the chair in front of the wall, the other one would shoot to see who came closest to the head. They took one shot at a time with a.22 pistol. We asked them where the gun was and they said in the kitchen. We found it and arrested the man who shot the other one, and charged them both with intoxication. An ambulance was called. The gun was put in evidence. People – Alcohol – Stupidity plus add a gun…………….it is mind-boggling.

During one of our times together, Doug and I were sent on a call with Unit 15. John (The Animal) Ansenne worked 15 and he went up to Doug, grabbed him by the neck and told Doug, “come here, I need to clean out my ears. You look like a Q-Tip with that long blond hair”. The command was always after Doug to get his hair cut. Animal continued to try to grab Doug and talking about ear cleaning. Doug was a good sport for a while but after a few times, Doug went after Animal with the MACE trying to spray him. The grabbing stopped but Doug was always Q-Tip to Animal.

One early evening, Bob and I were just finishing one of our great meals at 14’s Engine House when we got the call for a large disturbance. Bob was in the bathroom. I let him know what we had and that I would wait for him in the car. He came out and luckily when we got to the scene most of it was over. We talked to those involved and advised them as to dispersing and handling any problems a different way.

The 14’s Pumper pulled up and the Lieutenant came over and asked to talk to Bob. He came over and the Lieutenant opening up his fire coat and he was wearing

Bob's gun belt!! We thought you might need this. Having gone to the bathroom, Bob had taken the gun belt off and in the excitement of the large disturbance call; he had forgotten to put it back on. Luckily he did not need it and it was a good laugh for us all.

One night as it was getting dark, Bob and I got a call concerning a Break-In with an injured woman. Arriving at the scene, we were met by the fire crew. Stated they had been sent to assist an injured person. They said they found a woman with a bloody face. We checked the house for evidence that someone had entered the residence and found nothing. About that time, a young man arrived and said he was the woman's son. He asked why we were there and we told him what we knew. He said, "bull crap", my mother is a drunk. When she drinks and wants more, she attempts to get out of her wheelchair. She forgets she only has one leg and when she tries to walk she falls flat on her face. This is not the first time that she has done this. The son said, "He would take care of his mother" and we left.

Early afternoon, when Bob and I were working, we got a call for an Armed Robbery on Airport Highway at the Clark Gas Station. We were sent to assist U-13 on the call. We just happened to be closer than the other unit and were first on the scene.

Two black males with guns had come to the station and went inside. They pulled their guns and demanded money. The attendant gave them all that was in the register. They got into their vehicle and took off east on Airport Highway. Just as they got to the railroad tracks, a train was blocking their path, and before they could turn around, another train traveling in the other direction came by and blocked them between the two trains. There the bad guys sat. U-13 called and said a train on Airport stopped them and we told them to stay where they were – let the train pass and guess who they would find. Two males apprehended – two guns recovered along with all the cash from the hold-up. Good arrest for the good guys and too bad for the bad guys. If only "dumbest criminals" was on TV then and yes we did have TV in those days.

Doug and I were working and were sent to a man who had shot himself. It turned out as a suicide. We arrived and the man's wife met us. She said she saw her husband take a gun from the house and go into the back yard. After a few minutes she heard a shot and she ran to the rear yard. She found her husband lying on the ground and he was dead. He had shot himself in the head. We observed the male on the ground, with the gun as his wife stated and found the bullet not far from the body. 212 and coroner notified. Family was called for the wife. The wife had told us that her husband had been very despondent lately. Weapon was seized and placed in property room.

I think I mentioned before about having several ways to get out to our district, well this one day, Doug was driving and decided to take a totally new way. He says, "Let's use I-475 (which goes across the Maumee River around Perrysburg and Maumee) then gets off at Airport Highway. While on I-475 and a tad out of town, we get a flat tirc and I mean not just flat but shredded. No, we did not carry spare tires. OK, what do we do? We just happened to be at an exit that had a service station. We asked them, do you have and can we buy a used tire to fit this car? They did not have our size. We called dispatch, by phone, and explained our tire problem and where we were. He wanted to know "Why are you there?" We told him about our "new route to district".

He sent the city garage to fix the flat. We finally got to our district and were waiting for a command officer to show up for a legitimate explanation. No one ever said a word and of course we never used that "route" again.

Afternoons got busy and one early evening Bob and I were sent to a Prowler going through back yards. I was driving and we were traveling slowly on the street in question. Bob saw someone running in the back of a yard and he got out and gave chase. As I followed, attempting to head off the suspect, both Bob and suspect were jumping over fences. I heard a loud, "AAHHH". I stopped the car and as I was getting out, Bob came from one of the yards. He was holding his forehead. What happened was he had forgotten to duck under a clothesline. He hit his head and knocked himself to the ground. The suspect got away. Other than being a little dirty and embarrassed, Bob was OK.

Late another afternoon, Bob and I were sent to a disturbance involving a juvenile. The parents had called us because their son was giving them a hard time. We asked what type of hard time and they told us, he won't do as we tell him. He refuses to do work around the house, refuses to do his homework, just to name a few things. So we told him that if he did not do what we asked, we would call the police and have him taken to jail.

We told the parents do not use the police to threaten your kids. We do not and will not take just any juvenile to jail. We are not here to scare yours or any other child. We have a hard enough time trying to get along with kids. We did talk with the kid and asked him to try to do what his parents want and tried to give him good reasons why.

We did tell him that he should never be scared of us and we would come at any time to help him.

We told the parents "Don't ever call the police again like this. Do your job as parents. It is your responsibility to bring up your children – not us". The sad part is that this type of thinking continues through the years – people make babies but don't want to raise them.

CHAPTER ELEVEN

NIGHTS

Nights began as usual with the in and out of driveways, checking for open doors at businesses, driving and more driving. While driving is hazardous in winter, it does help with business checks and prowler calls. With snow on the ground, fresh footprints are readily seen and followed. Just his footprints have captured many a bad guy in his own home.

During our many shifts of nights, we could spend the entire time with absolutely no calls from dispatch. I have to admit that I talked both Bob and Doug into having a "cook out" every so often. We used a throwaway grill. We would bring our steaks and whatever to eat with them. We would do a thorough check of the district and then find a location to heat up the grill. Once we ate, we immediately were back on district checking for activity.

I'm not sure if any other crews thought this up and we certainly did not tell anyone. Why spoil a good thing! We definitely would have had a lot of company and not enough steaks.

Later on nights, during the summer, Doug and I were north on Reynolds at the railroad overpass at Angola. We saw a flash of light and looked up. We saw a car "flying" at us. The car did a flip in mid air, landing on its roof. The roof flattened to the body of the car, which trapped the occupants inside. We notified dispatch requesting immediate assistance. We were unable to get anyone out. Once help arrived we were able to get the car turned upright. There were two males inside. The driver was dead; his head had been flattened into his jaw. The passenger had suffered a traumatic back injury.

Once we were able to inspect the vehicle, we saw that the hood had been torn off. We saw that a clothespin was used on the four-barrel carburetor to hold all four barrels open. We determined that more than likely they were drag racing on Angola and instead of running west, they were eastbound on Angola. Angola runs along the side of the railroad track (along the overpass) and makes a turn to the left ending at Reynolds. Needless to say that as fast as they were going, they could not make the turn and instead went off the road. The vehicle then struck a light pole, which was the flash we saw, and then went over the side of the road (overpass), turned over and landed on the roof. What a waste of life just for the thrill of speed. This was the first fatal we had in a very long time.

September of 1968 brought another Civil Disturbance. It began in the Dorr and Detroit area. We all worked twelve hour shifts though they did not assign three men to a car.

Actually there were not that many problems and most of them were stopped before they escalated.

Later in the month, I had a day-off pulled for a special duty. I worked all night at the Commodore Perry Hotel. This was during that year's presidential campaign and Hubert Humphrey was one of the men going around the country campaigning. He was staying at the hotel for the night. Numerous officers were assigned to assist the Secret Service to be security in the hotel. It was a long and boring night.

Nights brought us another attempted suicide. Doug and I were dispatched to a residence where a husband had found his unconscious wife sitting in the car, inside the garage. The garage door was closed and locked. The car was not running as it had run out of gas. The key was in the ignition in the on position. A rescue squad was at the scene to give medical help. She was taken to the hospital for treatment by an ambulance. The husband went with them to the hospital. He could not give any reason why she would have attempted suicide. He told us, "She was not having any problems and was not under doctor's care". 212 notified and a detective was sent to follow-up at the hospital. As with many of our cases, we never learned a final outcome. That is what law enforcement is like and when you work as a street officer so many times you are there at the beginning but never the end.

In April 1969, Doug and I had our "first" call to a home on Golden Rd. We were to be sent there a few more times during the next months. The problem involved the son at the location. The young man was 17 and refused to be home at a certain time. He refused to help around the house and just would not do anything he was asked. He had even assaulted his own parents on several occasions.

We advised the parents as to what to do and how to handle the problems. The father did say at one time, "I'll take care of problem, he is my son and our responsibility".

A couple months went by and Bob and I were sent to the same home. This time it was the "son" who called. When we arrived the son was standing on the porch with a bewildered look on his face. We asked him, "What's the problem?" He replied, "I can't get into my house. My key won't work. No one will answer the door and look, all my clothes are in these paper bags." We knocked and the father answered. We told him his son had called and he says he can't get in. The father's response was, "Today is his 18th birthday. He is now an adult. I am no longer responsible for him. We changed the locks so he can no longer come in." The father shut the door.

The "birthday boy's" mouth dropped open and the tears began to flow. He asked us "what am I going to do?" We both told him, "that's up to you". We told him that he might try to have a long talk with his parents but there was nothing we could do for him, he is now an adult and responsible for himself. We drove away with him standing on the porch. We never received a call back to Golden Rd. again.

One quiet night, Doug and I were dispatched to what was perhaps the worst call I had ever had. It was a violent murder. A man opened the door to the house. He was in a highly nervous state, and said "I went to get some burgers for us and when I got home I saw this!" He was pointing at his wife who was lying on her side on the floor. He said that she spoke and said "Help me". Then said nothing further. The one thing we noticed immediately was the house was extremely warm. I went to the victim and felt for a pulse. There was none. The body was cool to the touch. She was dead. We saw her head and face had numerous bruises and there were marks like the head had been hit with an object. There was a "rolling pin" on the floor next to the body. It appeared to be the most likely weapon used to assault her. The walls, ceiling, floor and furniture were all covered with blood.

The husband went into the bedroom and brought out his son, who had been home during the time he was gone. The child was about 3 or 4 years old. 212 was contacted and directed us to let no one in or out of the location until they arrived. We were told to "protect the scene". Our "district sergeant" arrived at the scene and was attempting to enter, but we told him, "no". He became a little angry with us for not letting him in, but "so be it". We were under the detective bureau orders. When two detectives arrived, the Sergeant came in with them, and he immediately told us to "put on your helmets and button your coats, you are out of uniform!" Guess he was still a little miffed because we wouldn't let him in. You do what you are told and that is still what goes on today in law enforcement. The curious can be "many of your own" and nothing can screw a crime scene worse than a bunch of cops just wanting to see gore.

We did find a "bag of burgers and fries" in the kitchen. After a hard and thorough investigation by the two detectives, the husband was arrested for the murder of his wife and for the "murder of the unborn child she was carrying". She was not just pregnant; she was full term and over due. It was a double homicide. We did go to court for his trial and he was found GUILTY.

During one night shift, Bob had wanted to meet with U-15 and talk to one of the partners. While they talked in

15's car, the other partner sat with me. I asked him, "have you ever been on Unit 16's district?" He said no, so I got the bright idea that I would show him around. Unit 15 got a call for a disturbance and through some skillful, fast driving, we arrived at the call at the same time. Partners changed and we hustled back to our district. A short time later we passed our district sergeant and he motioned for us to stop. He came over and looked at the front of our car. He told us to get out and come over to him. He then said, "I don't want to know how it happened or where it happened, just get it out of there!!!" We looked at the grill of our car and there was an extremely large bird of some kind mashed in the grill. We were able to get it all out and there was no damage. The only thing we could figure out was that when I was "flying" to meet U-15 at the call, I had creamed the poor thing.

Doug and I were dispatched to a "Burglary and Armed Robbery" – Suspect Gone. We found that the resident had come home and he walked into the house to the kitchen. He saw his wife who was tied to a chair and a man was behind her with a gun pointing towards him. The suspect told the husband to sit in a chair, and he was also tied up. The suspect told the victims, "I'll make a deal with you. Don't call the police and don't let me see this in the newspaper. Then, maybe, I'll see that you get your rings back." He fled the scene. The wife stated the suspect had broken in and surprised her. He was described as wearing a mask. 212 notified and a detective came to the scene. Besides the wedding rings, the suspect took a gold watch, cash and a P-38 Luger. We put out a broadcast giving what little we knew but did make sure everyone was warned he was now armed.

One snowy night, Doug and I were driving through the parking lot at LaVoy's Bar. We observed a group of men and women holding onto rear bumps of cars. They were being pulled through the snow. Several of them had cardboard boxes that they were standing on as they were being pulled. We had to stop them before some one got serious injured. Most of them agreed that it was dangerous and stopped. There were, however, those usual few with too much to drink that wanted to give us a hard time. They came to see the light once they were given their choices, leave with the others but not drive or go to jail". They chose correctly and went with their friends. Adults can be so stupid at times.

There was a bakery next to the bar and the owner (baker) would get there about 3:00 to 4:00 am to start making the donuts. One morning there was a large rock that had been rolled up to the front of his door. He had no idea how it got there – it was very large. While we were taking a report and helping, the baker told us that he was from Germany and had been in the German Luftwaffe. He told us (in his very strong accent) that if someone had done this is Germany they would have been sent to a concentration camp.

Doug and I were on nights and heading north on Reynolds near the city limits. We saw a red light flashing. Remember cops are curious creatures – we went to see what was happening. An Ohio State Patrolman had a vehicle stopped. We checked to see if he needed assistance. The driver started to fight with the OSP officer and we jumped in to help subdue the suspect. The driver was extremely intoxicated. The patrolman asked if we could help him so he could take the driver to jail. We called dispatch and was given the OK. Doug drove our unit and we put the suspect in the front seat of the OSP unit with me sitting directly behind him. This was a time prior to "cage cars" – there was nothing between front and back seat. We had him put is hands over and behind the seat (bucket style front seats) and I had hold of his hands by the handcuffs – holding him against the seat.

Things heated up the moment we headed out. The suspect says, "Fuck this, I'm getting out of here!" He put his feet on the dash, then the roof of the car and was then in the back seat with ME. I sat on him until we reached the police station out in the county. He refused to take the Breathalyzer so we then assisted getting him into a cell. As we were leaving Doug was not with us and I called for him. He yells back, "I'm here in the cell with the suspect." How that happened we still do not know. As we were getting Doug out, the suspect charged us. We were forced to Mace him. He then started banging his head on the bars so we had to subdue him and take him to a safer, secure cell – with no bars. Ok we did have my partner and as we started to leave again, we heard glass breaking. We looked back and the drunk had put his fist through a small, reinforced window in the door. He was then observed to be writing a name in blood on the walls of the cell. Ok, "what's next?" We then assisted the OSP officer in getting the suspect to the hospital for the cut hand.

At the hospital a nurse was attempting to clean his hand and he looked at her, called her some very nasty names. He then used his good hand to squeeze the cut hand and got blood all over the nurse. The doctor, who had arrived to sew him up, saw what he had done to the nurse. The doctor told our guy, "Just for that I am going to use the dullest needle I can find and you are not getting "anything for the pain". "OWW". Miraculously the problems stopped and after a thank you from OSP, we went back to district.

One comical call occurred when Bob and I were dispatched to a dinner-dance restaurant on Unit 15's district in Heatherdowns Blvd. We were met by the headwaiter at the entrance and he pointed to a man on the dance floor. He said the man was drunk and refused to leave the dance floor. He had also been asked to leave the restaurant but refused. He was trying to get different women to dance with him but they were all refusing. We both went up to the "dancer" asking him to come with us, as we needed to talk. We took hold of his arms and then he started to fight. The three of us ended up on the dance floor as we tried to get the cuffs on him. During the entire time, the band continued to play, not missing a beat!! Once we got him outside, we called for a wagon to transport. He was charged with intoxication, disturbance and resisting arrest. While waiting for the wagon, a couple came by us. As they passed the suspect asked them, "You'll be my witnesses, won't you?" The man replied, "Yes" and here is my business card, as he put it in the man's shirt pocket. We knew the witness was an off duty detective. We all laughed and we never did go to court on this one.

One night shift, after roll call, Bob was driving us out to district. His favorite way to go was out Dorr St. He did his usual thing and drove slowly through the area, calling out to people along the way. He would say "Hi and thanks for all the info you gave us". They would look at him and ask, "Are you talking to me?" It was fun watching their reactions and reactions of others who were listening.

We then got a call of a Silent Alarm at an auto parts store on Dorr St. We arrived at the scene with another unit. They took the rear and we had the front. We had parked our cars so the headlights lit up the whole front of the store –inside and out. We could see two men inside and when they saw us, they became very excited and starting running through the store. They knocked things off shelves; they ran into tailpipes, which were suspended from the ceiling. The pipes knocked together making quite a musical tune for us. We just watched and laughed. Once the storeowner arrived, we went inside and arrested them.

We contacted 212 and the suspects were transported and ultimately charged with Burglary. On our way back to district, Bob had to drive the same way talking to the guys on the street corners. He would get a response like, "Why are you talking to me, I don't know you." He would call back "That's okay, we'll talk later." That night was busier than normal.

We got a call to check a home to check on a man's safety. The wife had awakened, and her husband was not in bed with her. She got up to look for him and found him lying on the floor in the hallway. We checked and he was dead. She told us that he was under a doctor's care since his last heart attack. 212 was notified and after advising that there was a medical condition and no signs of violence, the coroner was not sent nor a detective. We stayed with the wife till family could arrive.

Another night with Bob, we observed a vehicle pull out of LaVoy's swerving a little. We pulled the vehicle over and the driver got out explaining this was not his car. It belonged to the lady who was in the front seat with him. We asked her, "Why aren't you driving?" She told us that she had a few too many drinks. She added that she had wanted to drive but the man had said he would drive her home. We asked him, "Is that true?" He answered, "Well yah. Look everyone in the bar had a date when they left.

She was the only one still in the bar. What was I going to do?" The lady, who owned the car, was in a wheelchair. We had concerns as to the situation and her condition. We told them that we had a plan, which they would follow. I had the driver get in with me and Bob drove the lady's car. We took them to an all night restaurant. They were told to drink some coffee, maybe eat something, and then go and do whatever they were going to do. Hey, why not, we can be romantic, though, we wanted her to have time to make sure he was the "right choice".

One night Doug and I were sent to a disturbance at the White Hut. There were some juveniles inside causing trouble and refusing to leave. We entered and ordered them all out. One of the young men was not happy about it and put his fist through the plate glass door, severely cutting his hand and arm. He was pumping blood with every heartbeat – he had hit an artery. Rather than wait for an ambulance, Doug applied a tourniquet to the arm. I drove lights and siren to the nearest hospital. We notified his parents once we got there. They told them what he had done, also that he was ultimately responsible for the damage. His father got a little hot about it. We told him to he needed to blame his son for being so reckless. He's the one responsible for his actions, not us.

Another night, Doug and I were sent to a Silent Alarm at Rogers High School. We found a broken window on the rear side of the school. We asked dispatch for back up. We made entry and once inside drew our weapons. We started to check all the rooms. Ahead of us we saw a light moving around a room. We then saw a male with a flashlight leave the room. He saw us and threw a hunk of flat iron at us. In the same motion, he then raised his hands in the air to give up. We handcuffed him. We then made sure he was alone, and no other suspect(s) were involved. We then put our guns back in our holsters. When back up arrived, we transported the suspect to 212 for questioning and booking. We were asked if we wanted to add any charges as he had thrown the hunk of iron at us. We told them no, we weren't hurt. He has enough problems.

END OF JULY 1972

All things come to an end, as did our time on Unit 16. After all those years – for me seven, Bob just over five and Doug just under five – our unit was changed. We had tremendous times working together – did a lot of fun things – things we can't talk about – made many friends in the district. In fact, when residents started finding out we were leaving; they wanted to start petitions to keep us there. We thanked them for being so nice but it was probably time for a change. We were broken up as a unit, each being assigned to another district. So long Bob and Doug. It was great times. Since Bob and I are still good friends, he has helped me with many of these memories. Thanks, Bob!!

CHAPTER TWELVE

The new district was Unit 10 and new partners – Officer Tony Buller (salt) and Officer Hugh Marlin (pepper), thus we were a salt & pepper crew. Our district covered Bancroft, Delaware, Cherry, Monroe and Detroit Ave. It is much smaller than Unit 16 and was considered the inner city. There were more people living in the district. I knew this would be a totally different district. On Unit 16 we only had a few summons, subpoenas and warrants, where on Unit 10 we had piles the size of books.

You learn very quickly the difference in the people. Here when you asked if someone knew someone – the answer could almost always be "no" or "I never heard of them" or the best being, "I know them when I see them". Very few want or will cooperate with you as a cop. The uniform made it much harder to find wanted subjects.

What a difference in the amount of calls!! There were many days that as soon as you "hit on with the dispatcher as being in-service", you never stopped.... You ran from one call to the next. Too bad, if you were hungry. You learned quickly the "cop method of eating" – basically you inhaled your food. Both my wife and I, to this day, still eat as though a "call" will be broadcast. Many officers developed stomach problems because of this and "fast food" was a staple. A donut and coffee can be mobile. Hamburger and fries is quick and can also ride along. The mere fact of being a cop brings on the weight problems. Quiet, slow days were few and far between.

I lost track of all the reports we took involving assaults, armed and unarmed robberies, and B&E's. We had three hospitals on our district and spent a lot of time at them taking reports.

One afternoon, Hugh and I, were sent on a disturbance at one of the hospital's ER room. A very large male had walked inside and he started yelling. He was asked to leave but refused. He started to curse at the doctors and nurses. He refused to leave when we asked him and as I described he was "really large". We barely managed to get him outside and we had a hard time getting cuffs on him, as his wrists were big. The cuffs just barely fit. As we attempted to place him in the back of the patrol car, which were now equipped with shields between front and rear, he started kicking us. I took out my Mace and sprayed him. He did get maced but so did Hugh and I. It would seem that the seal on the rim of the can had sprung a leak and sprayed everyone around. We could hardly see so we just shoved him into the backseat and closed the door.

The prisoner continued being combative and was yelling from the back seat. We called dispatch and asked for a transport for the prisoner. Once they arrived we went back into the hospital and had them flush our eyes. Mace really burns. We later met with the transport crew and they told us that when we had closed the rear door to our car, the suspect's foot was trapped between the door and shield. Oh well, too bad, he shouldn't have resisted was our answer.

While working on U-10 with Tony, we made up a game one-day while checking out the rear of businesses in the alleys. We noticed there were a lot of beer and pop cans lying around. Well you need something to break up the monotony, so we made up what we called "canning". We would see how many cans we could run over. We gave ourselves a certain amount of alleys for each. We then kept score for each driver and we never ran out of cans to crush. Hugh never did really get excited about our little game.

Tony and I had a disturbance call involving a male in a second floor apartment. He was fighting with others in the apartment building. He refused to calm down. We knew as soon as we left, it would start up again. We arrested and cuffed him and as Tony was leading him out, I went to close all the doors to the apartment. I heard Tony call for help. The suspect was attempting to push him down the steps with his body. As I got to them, the suspect started kicking at us. I maced him and that seemed to quiet him down for a moment. We got him down and to the street. We called for a wagon for transport. We added a charge of resisting along with the disturbance.

One quiet Sunday morning, Hugh and I were sent to one of the hospitals on an assault. We talked to a middle aged man, who had come to the emergency room. It seemed that his wife had found him in bed with another woman. The wife had a knife and she attempted to cut off his

penis. He was able to make his getaway and made it to the hospital.
There were several deep cuts on his penis. While making out our report, we asked the victim if he wanted to "prosecute?" He said, "No". He was more worried about losing his penis!

There was one specific house that we spent a few times taking disturbance calls. The home belonged to a family that was well known to all the police – the "Biglers". Talk about crazy people. Whenever we were at the house, the mother would always have a bowl in her hands, mixing something. We said to ourselves, she was making "roach biscuits". The reason we thought that was when you looked at the walls they were moving. One time while there, one of the sons asked us to look at his shoes and see how shinny they were. Yah, we told him they really are shinny. He went and sat down putting his feet up on a table and we both started laughing. He did not have any soles on the bottom of the shoes – just the heels. In all their glory – we could see his filthy socks.

Another re-visit to our special place, a neighbor upstairs had called. Upon entering we saw another one of the Bigler Family sons, Venny. He smelled of intoxicants. The neighbor who called came down. We asked what we could do and he pointed at Venny, stating that Venny had come up and knocked on his door. He said that when he answered, Venny asked, "Would you make love to me?" The neighbor stated he punched Venny in the face and Venny fell down the steps. The caller went back upstairs and we arrested Venny for intoxication. We did stop by the hospital to have him checked for injuries due to the fall. There were none and he was booked.

Back to normal police work, Tony and I were dispatched to another disturbance at a home where the male resident met us at the door and said his name was Bishop Smith and this was his church. OK, Bishop what can we do for you? He pointed at a man and he explains that he brings men into his church to help them change their ways. All the time he is talking with us, the Bishop is slapping the top of one hand with the palm of the other. The Bishop goes on to explain that this man would not do as he asked. He still comes in drunk and today he came back here with a woman. I made the woman leave. At this point, the Bishop tells us, "Now I want this mother fucker out of my church!!" OOOOKKK, we asked the man to leave, and he did. The Bishop thanked us. We told him to call at any time should he have problems.

I have to admit that I had to feel sorry for some of the people who lived in our area. One call we had was an elderly lady saying she had saved her money to buy a used TV. When she had bought one, she went next door to get a neighbor to show it to her. When they returned and entered the house, they heard the back door close. Someone had come in and stolen her TV. How low can you get? There were so many nice, law-abiding people, who only wanted to survive and be happy in their homes.

We had another family, who had spent a lot of money and time, to improve the house and property. He had replaced the front fence, planted grass and replaced the front screen door. He had worked on many other improvements. The family had been gone for most of a day and when they came back they found someone had knocked down the fence, tore up the lawn and pulled off the screen door. The man told us that he knew he could not move away from the area, so he had wanted to make what he had as nice as he could for his family. This is what I get from my neighbors; they don't want us, or anyone, to have a nice place. All the residences around him were in rundown conditions. We had no answers for him but we did feel for him.

Our district did not have many good places to eat except we did have a Big Boy Restaurant and a wonderful Jewish Deli. They had the best-corned beef sandwiches in the entire city. Late one afternoon Tony and I went to the Big Boy to get something to eat. He was only inside for a couple minutes, when he came out to get me. There was a drunk inside who was giving the waitresses a hard time. We ask him to leave; he refused and started to shove us. We arrested him and as we escorted him out, the drunk said, "I want my food, I paid for it." Too bad buddy, with your attitude, you just missed out. We booked him for intoxication and disturbance.

At the end of May 1973, Tony was transferred to another district. I had an enjoyable 10 months working with him, so long Tony. Our new partner was Officer John Harpe. He started with us in June 1973. The three of us worked Unit 10 for two more months. In August we were assigned to a new unit – Unit 7 – we were now a wagon crew. Unit 7's district was just north of 10's. Since it was a neighboring district we had the same type of calls except we would transport other crews arrests.

One morning, my partner John wanted to get something to eat. He wanted to go to the Deli. I got my usual "corned beef sandwich" and he said he wanted something different. He said that everyone had been telling him to get "lox". I told him he would not like it. Being a tad hardheaded, he said he would still try it. As I was eating, I looked over at him and he looked at me, saying – "Dan, it's still alive. I can't eat this." We got a doggy bag and once outside he threw it away in the first garbage can we found. I told him but he wouldn't listen.

Near the end of August 1973, the police department was going to try something different. They were going to make all the outer districts into one-man cars, thus you would have two one-man cars per district rather than one car with two men. I thought the change might be good and I put in for the training and got it. The districts they were changing were 15, 16, 18, and 19. I was assigned to the district, which had been 18 but was now split into 181 and 182. After a week of special training I became 182. So long to Unit 10, Unit 7, and to my partners for the past year, they were all great to be with and I would never have hesitated to partner with them again.

CHAPTER THIRTEEN

SEPTEMBER 1973

My new district is Unit-18; it is located in the northwest part of the city, with much of it touching the Michigan state line. This should help to make things interesting. Our district is almost as large as Unit-16. My two partners are Officers "Matty" and "Pfeif". They were both originally police officers in Maumee, Ohio. Maumee and Toledo touch each other at the southern tip of Toledo. They both had to test for Toledo and were required to attend the Academy. It is not like television or movies, where all you do is show up and start working in another department or state. We do have a "real world".

One thing for sure, there was a lot of traffic out there and that meant a lot more "traffic accidents". It is noted that now the term is "traffic crash", nothing is considered an accident. We originally started working as a 2-man unit, though when they used the one-man cars – we were then called 181 and 182. Our first month was on the afternoon shift as Unit 18. When we transitioned to days, were one-man cars. Returned to afternoons and became Unit 18. The administration was testing the concept of men working alone. After several shift changes, we finally ended up working one-man through Days, Afternoons and Nights. I am now permanently U-182.

One of the most difficult things working alone on a night shift is "staying awake". My pet saying was "nights were made for sleeping and loving". Working nights I got very little of either. Many officers prefer certain shifts and they can handle the "sleeping during the day". Up to retiring and still today, I must sleep at night or it is like being in la la land the next day. I knew immediately that on slow nights I would be getting out of the car many times and checking things on foot, just to stay awake. The other problem for me was I have never liked "coffee", yah eaten donuts – but no coffee. That didn't help during nights.

We introduced ourselves to the firefighters in our district – 23 Firehouse on Laskey Road. Again, they were another bunch of great guys. We found out that they were also excellent cooks. You know what that meant, more great meals. Actually we found out a short time later, the firemen had called their buddies at #14's Firehouse to check on us and they were told that we were pretty good guys. It was nice to hear that, maybe we should have had recommendation letters made up?

It was nice to find that we did not have anywhere near the amount of warrants or summons to serve in that district.

AFTERNOONS

My first two afternoons were with Jim Matty and Ron Pfeif. I did feel that we would make a great working crew. The first two afternoons were very quiet, and the next two with Pfeif were busy. Our first call was a Grant Theft from a TV Store, located on Tremainsville Rd. The owner told us that two black males had entered the store and while one kept him busy, the other suspect grabbed both a color television worth $550.00 and a tape player worth $200, making it a grand theft of $750.00. They fled east on Tremainsville in a tan station wagon with no plates. Did our usual notifications and made a report. The month continued with many reports involving various crimes, including thefts from vehicles.

During the month, Pfeif and I had two separate "exposings" reported to us. The first involved a young white male, who had approached a stopped car at a red light. He knocked on the driver's window and asked the female driver, as he licked his lips, "do you want to play with me?" At that point he pulled out his penis. He then ran and got into a green two-door Chevrolet and drive off. Again there was no license plate number. Later the same evening, a suspect matching the same description was hiding in some bushes and as a woman walked by, he jumped out with his pants down, and asked, "do you want to watch me jack off?" She told him no and left, leaving him standing with his pants down. She called as soon as she got home and we made out the two reports. We notified 212 and put out a general broadcast alerting area officers as to the suspect and his MO.

Ron and I had an interesting call during the same period. We were sent on a disturbance at a bar on Secor Rd. near the Michigan state line. There was a male inside creating a disturbance. The bartender had ordered him to leave, and of course, he refused. We arrived and attempted to have him leave. He said, "I'm am FBI agent." We asked for his ID, and he immediately pulled out his Social Security Card. We immediately placed cuffs on him. He was arrested and transported to jail. On the way downtown, he started to yell at us. He told us that when he got out of jail, he was going to beat both of us up. About half way downtown, I stopped the car on the side of the expressway. I got out, walked to the back door, opened it and told him, "OK I'm going to take the handcuffs off and then you can beat us up!" He started crying and refused to get out. I got back in and continued to drive to the jail. He again started yelling and telling us that he was going to beat us up once he got out. I just kept driving and when we got to the jail, and were getting ready to get him out and he started crying again. He refused to get out of the car.

We were at a point of having to physically pull him out when one of my old partners happened to come to the jail also. Doug asked us, "What do you have there?" We told him about our would-be fighter. Doug walked over to the car and said something to the "prisoner", and the prisoner sheepishly got out of our car. We thanked Doug and took the prisoner in the jail where he was booked for intoxication. We were heading back to district, when dispatch called and told us to phone "254", the jail number. I called and they told us, "Remember the man you just left us? He is now banging his head against the bars of the cell." I could hear him banging his head in the background. The jail told us we had to come back and take him to the hospital "safe keeping". I told the jail that he had been just fine when we left and hung up on him. They did not call us back.

I began working alone as U-182. I had many house watches (people on vacation) and numerous accidents. One-man cars always watch out for each other. Any time 181 got a call, I would drive by to check for his safety or see if he needed assistance. He would do the same thing. Dispatch would always send both units on calls such as disturbances, fights, in process calls, where you would normally use a 2-man unit. Remember also, the adjoining units would also manage to "drive by" if they were not already on a call. You protect your own….

Ron and I were sent on a disturbance at a home one morning. The woman, who answered the door, stated "her husband had been up all night drinking in his chair" and he was still sitting there. There were many empty beer cans around the chair and he smelled of alcohol. We told him he was under arrest and he help up a 7-Up can, telling us to look inside the can. I told him, "I don't care what's in the can." We literally had to hold him up to get him out of the house and into a wagon we had called for transport.

NIGHTS

Spent many nights without being dispatched to any calls. I would get out of the car and walk around buildings trying to stay awake. I did get a few drunk drivers with both my one-man partners. You spend those times looking for things out of the ordinary, burglaries in progress, prowlers, any one out at a time that made them suspicious. Those were very long nights.

One particular summer night, Ron and I were sent to check out a suspicious car. It had been seen driving through a neighborhood, with its lights off. No description of the vehicle was given. The neighborhood was on a street, which ran circular. Ron went to the right and I went to the left, with both of us turning our lights off. We both were driving slowly and a short time later Ron got on the air and said, “I’m hit”. The suspect had gotten out of his vehicle and left it in drive. The car continued moving and struck Ron’s car. There was only light damage. We never did locate the suspect and ultimately found that the car he left was stolen. We had it towed and protected for prints. Never did find out if a suspect was identified. This was back in the time when prints had to be classified and then “hand searched”….AFIS would not be invented until many years later, and yes, we did not have a clue as to what DNA was yet.

Near the end of 1975, my two partners put in for transfer to other jobs in the department. They had both wanted to do other types of police work and a larger department, like Toledo PD, did have a variety of assignments. It had seemed that I had more exciting calls with Pfeif than with Matty, but that is the way it happens. That is not to say that we did not do a lot or have a good time doing what we did. It is the nature of law enforcement – feast or famine…. lots of excitement or dull as hell.

So long to my partners, Jim and Ron, great working with you and the best to you both.

CHAPTER FOURTEEN

DAYS 1975

Not sure who my partners will be on U-181. There were several who were assigned to fill in for a couple months at a time, though nothing permanent.

In 1975 the department start a program to "try and keep all officers in shape". I was one of the many who took advance of the program. It was held at "Holy Spirit Seminary" gymnasium on Airport Highway. I used to run outside when weather permitted but then used the inside track the other times. After running, I would get into a basketball game with the other officers. Well, during one game, as I came down from getting a rebound, my landed on my left leg. It gave out and I went straight to the floor and could not get up. Nothing was broken, however, I had torn all the ligaments and tendons around the knee. So much for "keeping in shape!". The orthopedic doctor did not operate but had me in therapy using weights. He did not release me back to work until April 1975. I spend 87 days off duty. The only good thing was that it was "job related" therefore I did not lose my sick time.

One of my first days back, I had a DOA of an elderly man who had passed away in his sleep. His wife had gone to wake him up and he failed to respond. She called the rescue squad but he was already dead when they arrived. They called for an officer and when I arrived I checked for any signs of violence on or about his body. There was none. He had been in poor health. I notified 212 and again advised them there would be no need for a detective. I remained with the wife until a relative arrived.

Ah yes, on a personal note, in July of 1976 I had my first bout with a kidney stone. It was removed surgically as it would not pass on its own. Learned quickly what "real" pain can be. I was off work for over a month. At that time we had "replacement badges" and I now became #232, moving up in seniority.

February 77, I again had problems and had emergency surgery for gall bladder. It had apparently almost ruptured. I was off work another month and finally came back "light duty". I was in the Record Bureau for two "terribly long" weeks. Finally, back on the road and it was great. It is a help through that bigger departments do allow "light duty positions" rather than having to eat up all the sick time or go without pay. It helps though some of the positions can be very boring and confining.

AFTERNOONS

Back on afternoons I had a report of another exposing. An elderly lady stated she was sitting in her car at a stop sign. A white male in his 20's came up to her side of the car and asked her "where is the nearest Baptist Church?" He then pulled his pants down, pulled out his penis and began playing with it. He asked her, "Do you want to play with it?" She told me she sped off, leaving him standing in the street. I put out a description and made the report.

Near the end of April 1977, I had the opportunity to be an Acting Sergeant. This would be one of many times during the next two to three years. There had been a test given for Sergeants however there was some type of lawsuit going on, so no one from that list could be chosen. I had taken the test but had not placed very high on the list. The administration decided to use "the seniority list" for now and asked officers to fill in sergeant positions when they were open on a daily basis. I took advantage of the requests as it did mean more money for those days and as a Sergeant you usually had four districts to supervise. The Sergeant responds with the officers on calls that required multiple officers.

We began getting a lot of student riders through the criminal justice program at Toledo University. This would continue throughout the year. Also we would have riders who were officers just out of the recent academy. We were also getting more female officers during the early 70's. I would have well over a dozen different riders over the coming months.

One afternoon in May, my district was "pulled". I was assigned to work Unit 4 Wagon with Officer Bill Nendricks, who went through the academy with me. Unit 4's district was just north of downtown. We had one interesting call involving a check for a possibly demented woman. We found the woman in a high state of anger. She was yelling and hitting at anyone coming near here. She attempted to spit on everyone. The callers had said the woman had been refusing to take her "meds" and now they could not find her medications. They thought she had thrown them away. Her doctor had been called and he had advised them to take her to the hospital to be admitted for "safe keeping". We got her calmed down and she went with us to the hospital.

Once there, all "hell broke loose". The doctor came in and tried to talk with her and she began to spit and hit him. She spit and hit the nurse. She began trying to bite everyone. The doctor told us, "She needs to be taken to the State Mental Hospital". Ok, we go out and get our portable stretcher and managed to get her strapped down. We put a breathing type apparatus over her mouth so she could not spit (this was way before the professionally made spit guards that are now available to law enforcement) – this was the day of "make do with what you can find". I was lucky; it was my turn to drive, so guess who got to sit in the back with our "patient", my partner Bill. We arrived at the state hospital and were told to wait until a staff doctor came to exam our lady. After a period of time we saw someone walking towards us. It was a man with a very long ponytail, a backpack with an antenna attached to it. He walks up to the nurse and asked, "What is the problem". The nurse tells him this is the lady brought in for safekeeping.

At that point we figured he was the doctor and proceeded to tell him what had happened and what the doctor at the hospital had told us. He then reaches down and takes off the "breathing apparatus" the other doctor had given us and she starts up again. She began cursing and spitting at him. The doctor tells us that she just needs to calm down and we left, telling them – she's all yours.... We laughed all the way back to district.

In January 1978 the city was hit by a "blizzard". Snow, snow and more snow. The only way for me to get to work was to be picked up by someone with a 4-wheel drive vehicle. The city was entirely impassable. Once at work we were assigned as a two-man crew. We were given brand new "Jeep Wagoneers" to drive, which were donated by the Jeep Plant in Toledo. Jeep's main manufacturing plant is in Toledo, Ohio. They worked great for us during the snow emergency. We had them for four days until the street crews could get the roads open. We were then back to business as usual.

NIGHTS

September 1976 I had another kidney stone and was off until the last of October. Too much calcium again caused the stone. I had tried to stay away from anything with calcium in it but apparently had not been that successful.

Nothing of great interest happened until September of 1977. I was involved in another accident. It occurred as I was traveling east on Alexis Rd. I observed a car coming toward me in my lane of traffic. I was unable to move into another lane as the lane to my right had traffic. Also the two lanes, to my left, on the opposite of the road were filled. All I could do was stop my car and immediately hit my overhead red lights and wait. She kept coming and I was struck head on. I got out to check the other driver, who was a woman. She was highly intoxicated, and she asked me, "Why did you hit me?" Needless to say I arrested her and took her in for the intoxilyzer. Her vehicle was towed. Neither of the vehicle had major damage and no injuries thankfully.

A few nights later, I was sent to a one car accident on Laskey Rd at the intersection of Douglas & Tremainsville – a three-way intersection. It was a sight to behold. Sitting on top of two large, round, rubber traffic posts, was a vehicle. The posts were used as road dividers on Laskey. Normally if a car strikes them, it will bounce off. The driver was not drunk. The driver told me that he had wanted to find out what would happen if he hit them and he found out. He had been traveling at a high rate of speed to manage to go up and land on top of the posts. What an idiot! He was cited for Operating without Due Regard. When the tow truck pulled the vehicle off, it also took the oil pan, muffler and tail pipe. What gets into the minds of these people?

In July 1978, I traveled again out west with my family for vacation. We spent time with our good friends in Orange, California. My wife Kathy had worked with "Judy" when she lived there for a while. We were on our last day, on the road, heading home and Kathy said she was having a terrible headache. She took some aspirins that we had but it only helped for a short time. As soon as we got home, I took her to our doctor and he felt she was a bad migraine. He gave her some medication that helped. He did tell her that if it continued he would order tests for her.

Everything seemed to improve. About ten days later, the 9th of August, the pain returned. I took her to the doctor again and he took one look at her and told us to go straight to the hospital. He told us that he was going to let the hospital know we were on our way.

Kathy said she wanted to stop at home to get some personal things. The doctor told her, "I want you to go straight to the hospital, NOW!" When we got there, the staff was waiting and they took her directly to intensive care. Tests were ordered immediately. I called my mother, asking her to come and stay with the kids. I stayed with Kathy the rest of the day. I went home in the evening and during the night I got a phone call to immediately get to the hospital, as there was a change in Kathy's condition. I woke the children and told them where I was going. I told them I would let then know as soon as I found out what was happening.

When I got there, I was told she had gone into a convulsion and was in a coma. They were calling in a specialist. After the tests were made, it was found that she had a deep brain hemorrhage, caused by an aneurysm that had burst. I was told that the only thing we could do was wait, and see what developed. She would either improve or not. The next couple days went by so slowly and all I could do was sit by her side and pray.

I was told her condition had worsened and she was brain dead. It was now only a matter of time before she would die. The only thing keeping her going was the life support machine. They told me that in the end it would not help. She had only a day or two left. All I could do was sit and watch her lose her life. Our daughter, Julie, had come to the hospital to be with her mother and me. I again talked to the doctors and they told us she had only a few hours left. I went to do some thinking and made the most difficult decision of my life. I went back and told them to take her off the machine and let her go with dignity.

I'm sure that is how she would have wanted it. A priest was with us, to give her last rights. Julie and I watched her leave us, August 14, 1978. I had just lost my wife of twenty years and I never really knew how much I loved her until that moment. I have always regretted that I was unable to tell her that I loved her one more time.

I now had to go home and tell our two sons, Mike and Doug, that their mother was gone. I began the process of notifying relatives and family friends. Our good friends, the Lavan's, we had just visited in California also came to the funeral. After the funeral, alone at home that evening, I got a phone call.

The caller said, "Dan, how are you doing?" It was from Officer Lee Beese. Just over a month before, Lee had also lost his wife. She was shot and killed in a hold-up where she worked. I have to admit, I broke down and cried. We talked for a long time. I have never forgotten what he did. I can only guess how hard it had to be for him to call. I hope that Lee knows how much that call meant and how much it was appreciated.

After a couple more days off, I went back to work. The department, rather than letting me go back to work alone, assigned me to dispatch until the end of the month.

How much was this going to change my life? Everything was now up to me and I am now a single parent of three.

CHAPTER FIFTEEN

A NEW BEGINNING – MY LIFE WITHOUT KATHY AND THE KIDS WITHOUT THEIR MOTHER

I know that I have to become more focused in coping with things that will be happening, especially in caring for my children. Until now, I never knew how much I depended on Kathy. You never realize how much responsibly each parent takes on.

One of the first things that I did was to give the kids some responsibility in running our home - the laundry, house cleaning, bathrooms, just to name a few. I felt that we all needed to keep busy and keep our minds occupied. Family, friends and fellow officers were extremely kind and compassionate to me. They had me go out to dinner, but after two or three times, I would tell them thanks and graciously try to bow out. I couldn't take always going home alone after the outings. It is hard to be the "third" person.

When I would work on the day and night shift, I would be home in the evenings with the kids. On afternoons, I had to work something out, so I could be there for them. I do admit in the beginning, I may have been at work but only in body not mentally.

DAYS

The day shift was the usual with assorted reports, few minor disturbances and accidents, with a few minor injuries. In November l978, I was able to trade shifts with another officer. He worked my afternoons and I worked his days. We were able to do this trade a total of four times. I was very thankful to the officer who traded with me, Officer Ellis.

The first trade, I worked with various officers, on their districts. The people we were involved with never changed, no matter what shift or what area, they all are alike. In December I was back on my regular shift and since it was the Christmas Season, I was called to transport many shoplifters caught at the Franklin Park Mall. It was snowy and the accidents were many. Why do people forget how to drive in snow? As December went on I was scheduled to work Christmas Day. My command called me in a couple days before and told me they had worked out a deal for me. They gave me Christmas Day off so I could be with the kids for our first Christmas alone. It was so thoughtful of them and you do learn quickly that "police are a family themselves". Thank you, guys!!.

Back to my trade shift again in March, and this time I was assigned to a crew, Unit-7 Wagon. I would always be assigned to that unit the next two trades. I had two new partners for the month I would be there and they were two good men.

One morning we had a kind of high-speed chase. Trust me, it is not quite the same chasing someone in a wagon. I was not the driver this time and being passenger can be a little nerve-racking. We did catch him and he received a total of (8) citations plus a trip to jail and a vehicle tow. The month continued with warrants, reports and the normal run of the mill stuff.

One evening, while sitting at home, I got a phone call from my old friend and partner, Bob Bannon. "Dan, what are you doing?" "Get ready, I'm on my way to pick you up. Don't say no – just be ready". Well, I did go out with him. We ate, had a couple drinks and talked. Yes, it did feel good to get out. In fact, we did it a few more times. I needed it and thanks Bob, you were right. You still are a good partner and friend.

NIGHTS

January 1979 and I pray this will be a better year for all of us. Early in the month, I took a report of an assault by a fifteen-year-old girl. The girl had gotten into a heated argument with her mother. The girl actually beat up her own mother by striking her numerous times with her fists. The teen then ran away. The mother refused to go to the hospital for treatment. After notifying the Juvenile Bureau of the incident, I made out the report.

Later in the month, I observed a vehicle swerving all over the road, forcing other vehicles to get out of his way.

Luckily he did not strike anyone. After I was able to get him stopped, he could hardly stand up. He was highly intoxicated. I arrested him and towed his vehicle. I took him in for the "test".

There was an armed robbery at an all night service station. An older white male and approached the female attendant. He asked for some cigarettes, and when she turned to get them, the male said, "I'll take the money in the cash box too". She observed him holding a small gun in his hand. After giving the money, the male fled west from the station. Normal procedure was followed, called 212, broadcast a description and wrote the report.

I did have a sad call one night. I was sent to assist a lady, whose husband had just passed away. She stated that she had gotten out of bed to look for him and found him in his chair. She could not get him to respond. She called us immediately. I checked and the man was deceased. She told me that he had been taking heart medication. Notified 212 and advised that no follow-up would be needed. As I sat and waited with her, I told her that I knew what she was going through. She said, "How can you know?" I told her that I had just lost my wife a few months before. She looked at me, put her arms around me, saying, "I'm so sorry." And yes, we both started crying in each other's arms. After her family arrived, I was outside, alone in the car, trying to get my composure back. That was a tough one.

Back on my regular shift in April, I did have an interesting thing happen, that I had never seen in person before. I was assigned to do traffic around the area of the Jeep administration building. It was set to be demolished that morning. One minute I was looking at the large, multi-story structure, then boom-boom-boom, and the building collapsed onto itself. Could not believe how quick it happened.

May was night shift and I had another deceased male. Rescue Squad from 23's station house had tried to save him at the scene, but he did not make it. The man had had heart problems for some time and was on medication. This one he did not survive. Waited for relatives and wrote the report. As you have seen by now, police officers spend many hours helping people who are not victims of "crime". The first line in the oath of office is to serve and protect the community. Service comes in many forms and so often it is just being with those going through trauma and being a good listener. 70% of law enforcement has nothing to do with glamour and anything someone would make a movie about.

Later in the month I was sent on a call of a break-in at a location off my district. The suspect had left a note stating, "You can call the police if you want to, but I still can get into your house. It is easy to do. I know when you leave and return." 212 notified and a detective was sent to the scene and the report was filed. The regular district crew and I kept an "eye" on the home.

I was attempting to pull a car over which headed north on Secor Rd. I had my overhead lights on. He finally stopped near the Michigan border. As he stopped, a Michigan State Police car pulled up, asking if I needed any help. I thanked him but said no, I have him for drunk driving. The driver then spoke up and said, "I'm in Michigan, and you can't arrest me!" The Michigan officer told him, "So sorry, but no, you are still in Ohio". Actually, to be truthful, we were in Michigan by about 100 feet. I thanked the officer again, and proceeded to transport the driver for the test and booking. A minor 100 feet, who cares – he was still drunk driving and a hazard.

AFTERNOONS

Two things happened in June of 79, my son Doug got his driver's license and my daughter, Julie, graduated from the 8th Grade. While attending a party in the church hall, after the graduation, we sat at a table with one of her girlfriends, and her mother. While talking to the girl's mother, Karen, I asked her, "Would you like to go out with me some night?" Karen said yes. We did go out. All the time I was with Karen, I kept looking over my shoulder, thinking "Kathy" would find me cheating on her. It took me a while to ask her out again. We spent a lot of time together, and things did start to get serious and intimate. But, as time went by, thinking it was love; we (mostly me) knew something wasn't quite right. I, for one, was trying to re-live my life with Kathy. I knew if we ever got married it would not work out as it was doomed to fail. You can't have a marriage living in the past. I did something that I feel bad about to this day, I broke it off and in the process I know I hurt her. I hope in time she forgave me.

A couple times in June, I was assigned to work at the Inverness County Club directing traffic for the US Open Gold Tournament. Those were "long" days.

Another special assignment was to assist the Vice Squad with a drug search warrant at a suspected "drug house". I was one of two 1-man cars assigned. It was a house on my district. We were there to watch the suspects, making sure they did not interfere with the search. It was interesting watching the Vice "Dicks" search a house. They even took off the curtains on the windows. I asked them why and they told me that sometimes the drugs are diluted in water and then fabric (curtains) is used to absorb the drugs. The dopers then submerge them back in water for the next process of evaporating the liquid to pure drug. No matter how long you are a police officer, you continue to learn new things daily.

NIGHTS 1980

One night in 1980 a lady called for help. She told dispatch that someone was pounding on her front door. She said she had turned on the front light and saw a white male on the porch and he was asking for “help”. The man then collapsed on her porch. When I arrived I found him passed out cold. I called for a rescue squad from 23’s House. They called for an ambulance to get him to the hospital. No one could figure out what was wrong with him. I made a report but never did find out what actually had been the problem.

On September 20, 1980, I was dispatch Code 3 (lights-siren) to someone breaking into a home now!! I was traveling north on Douglas and as I approached Laskey, I had a red light. I had to come to a stop. I then proceeded across Laskey, I noticed a vehicle on my left and I stopped my car again, to let it pass. My overheads were still on and flashing. At that point, dispatch radioed a “cancel”. I was stopped and it was like slow motion as the car continued to come straight at me. He struck me to the left front driver’s door. The impact caved in my door up against my body. I had three broken ribs from the impact. I notified dispatch, telling them that I was involved in a crash and I was injured and was unable to get out of the car. #23 Firehouse responded to help me and once they saw who it was, I got better than the best of help. They had to force open the right front door to get at me. I told them to check on the other driver, and they said another crew was doing that. We are personally taking care of you. They transported me to the hospital and once there I thanked them. The doctor said that all they could do for the broken ribs was strap them and give pain medication. My partner on 181 came to the hospital and took me home. #181 was Officer Bruce Simmons and he would remain a partner for about 3 to 4 years. After being off a few days, I came back to work light duty again in Records. I ended up working a month and a half there before I was released back to the street.

Some time near the end of 1980, the department was "short" of uniformed officers on the street. Due to finances they were unable to have an academy. Detectives were re-assigned from the two bureaus – 212 and 257. The detectives, through the union, were given letters of assurance that once an academy was hired and on the street, they would be returned to their original assignments. Of course, the reassignments were made by "seniority", the least were transferred down to the shifts.

I was on midnights at the time and one of the detectives, who came onto our shift, was a female named Barb Zuelke. Little did I know at that time, the effects she would have on my life!! I had seen her around the building maybe a couple times but never met her. She was hired in October of 1972 but our paths never really crossed until 1980. Up to that time, I had continued to date but nothing serious. I had dated a couple of other female officers, though it was usually only one date. It still did not feel right for me to be with another woman. Barb was still only a face at roll call until later in 1981.

From January to July, I was given the opportunity to be an acting sergeant again, working the various sergeant districts. I would estimate I was acting about half the time. One particular afternoon in 81, I had a student ride with me. We only had two calls that day, but she got to see a lot. The first call was a "suicide". A man came home from work and found his wife sitting in her car in the garage with the motor running. He called for a rescue squad but she was already dead. Her husband was not able to determine why she killed herself. We stayed at the scene until the coroner and detective arrived. Her body was removed once they released the scene.

The next call was an assault. A woman reported her boyfriend had beaten her. #23 squad was at the scene when we arrived. The victim had already been transported to the hospital. We went to the hospital to complete a report. The student was impressed, saying, "I have never seen and known that people acted like this." I guess it opened her eyes to the real world.

On another afternoon, I was sent to a hospital to take a report of a female who had overdoes on pills. During my interview with her, she said, "All I wanted was love. I have a lot to give. All I want is someone to love me. I won't hurt anyone." She told me that her boyfriend had left her. 212 was notified and I put a "safekeeping" hold on her, for her own protection. Report was made.

DAYS 1981

Just after the first of the year, I started to notice the blonde lady officer, that was being assigned near my district, and sometimes as my partner on U-181, yes, that was Barb. We did answer a few calls together. One day I drove by as she was taking an accident report. As with any fellow officer, I drove by to see if she needed help. After she finished the report, we pulled into a park and talked. After a period of time, I got the nerve up and asked her would she like to have dinner some night. She accepted. (It took him an eternity to finally ask me out!!!- Note from the typist). We later went out, had a good time. First ate dinner and then went to a movie. It was a pleasant evening for me. I did not ask her out again for about two weeks (typist again: God what did I do wrong?)

Finally asked her again and then it never stopped from the second date. I felt something with her. As we continued to date we never flaunted our being together. Actually there were only a handful of officers that had any idea we were dating. In a department of 600 plus people, secrets are hard to keep.

As time went by, my feelings grew and there was no one else. I found that she was a loving and caring person. Yes, I was hooked on her.

In the meantime, my oldest son, Mike, got married on the same day that Doug graduated from high school. Yah, that was one busy day. I asked Barb to be my special guest at Mike's wedding and she accepted. Of course, she and my mother had to meet outside the church and from that point on became fast friends. I was doomed!!

The next month, July 1981, Doug, Julie and I headed west on a vacation. We visited our friends the Lavan's in Orange, CA. After leaving there, we drove to San Diego, and visited with one of my old partner's, Tony Buller. He had relocated to California after leaving the police department. We spent a couple days, and one night we had a cookout on the beach along the Pacific ocean. After everyone had eaten, I took a walk along the shore. I was listening to the ocean and thinking. Looking out at the ocean, I had some deep and serious thoughts about Barb. I made up my mind that when we got back home, I would ask her to marry me. As I knew then that I loved her and her alone!

I had called Barb a couple times while still out west but didn't say thing to her about my thought. When we got home I called her to let her know we were back. No sooner than I hung up the phone, she was pulling up out front of the house. Well, maybe not that quick but close to it. We went out later and it was then that I asked her to marry me and be my wife. I told her that I loved her for being who she was and she said yes, and she loved me also....

After talking a while, Barb said, "I have a confession to make." "What?"...I asked. She answered, "I have wanted to be with you for some time. I used to ask the Desk Sergeant, when possible, to assign me to any district close to Unit 182, yours." She was stalking me. That was before it was actually a crime - hey it worked. I have no complaints about her doing it.

Many plans had to be made. We picked the wedding date as April 16, 1982. We both wanted a "small" wedding. Yah, right!!! I have a very large family. Barb's was very small. We did want to invite some of the people she worked with in the Juvenile Bureau. Ok that would work, and then we thought about the people we worked with on the street. Ok again, well..............we ended up with around 300 people at our reception. Relatives, friends, firemen from 23's Firehouse and it grew. My mother paid for the band, a well-known Polish Band that traveled throughout the Midwest and East Coast. Great food and drink and a good time had by all. We actually had to rent the National Guard Armory to house everyone. Yes, we did invite the guardsmen, who were on duty, that night - a few were cops. The Lavan's came from Orange.

One thing I wanted was for us to have a new home to start our life together. I did not want Barb to come into our marriage to a home someone else had made. This is a comment for anyone reading this book – you must have a fresh start and a new beginning with nothing from the past to haunt you. I made sure we bought a new home for our new beginning.

Friday, April 16th, 1982, Barb and I married. It was a happy day for both of us. We spent the night alone in our new home. The next day, everyone and everything was moved in. I told the kids that Barb was not here to replace their mother. She was my wife and I love her. All I asked of them was to respect her as my wife. If in time they grew to love her, she would be happy to have their love. Later the next week we went on our honeymoon.

We went to Las Vegas, and yes, I made a big mistake. She loved the place and got the gambling bug. We do in the future go back many times.

A NEW BEGINNING AND END OF SECTION ONE

POLICE
229

TOLEDO POLICE

263
The Blade

POLICE
276

PART TWO

A NEW BEGINNING

CHAPTER SIXTEEN

There are now two Palicki's on the Toledo Police Department. Barb is assigned to Unit 82, a one-man car, and I'm still Unit 182. We are about four districts apart, and this could get interesting. I now have someone to worry about when she is dispatched to calls, even though I know she can take care of herself. We ride to and from work together and are able to talk about how we took care of our different calls. We were able to vent our frustrations, as we both had experienced the same issues. This brought us even closer together.

About a month after we were married, Barb told our son, Mike, to move back home. We had a fourth bedroom, and he was told it was his. Mike had gone through a short marriage and had lots to deal with. Barb told him that he shouldn't be alone at a time like that. Like I said, she is a loving and caring woman.

NIGHTS

November 1982, the newest Police Academy graduates came to the street! I had some of the rookies ride with me most of the month. Most of them seemed to be ok and will make good officers, both men and women.

In March 1983, our son, Mike, rode a couple times with me. He was thinking about becoming a police officer. I think he enjoyed riding and what and how we did things.

Later the same month, our daughter, Julie, rode with me and I believe it really opened her eyes just that one night. We had a disturbance at an apartment. The woman's ex-boyfriend was refusing to leave. He also refused to leave when I asked him. I gave him a choice – go on your way or you'll go to jail. He charged at me and after a short tussle, I subdued him. After cuffing him, I decided to transport him myself, rather than calling for a wagon. I wanted Julie to see how people were booked into jail. The entire trip downtown he was in the rear seat kicking the shield, cursing at me and telling me that when we got to jail he was going to kick me when I tried to get him out. I called our dispatcher, asking to have someone meet me at the jail for assistance. As I pulled up, I had two deputies waiting outside. As I opened the rear door to get him out, he kept his promise and tried to kick me. As he was going at me, the two deputies opened the other door and grabbed his hair, pulling him out to them. He had to be physically dragged inside the jail. Once inside, the man began spitting at the female deputy who was trying to take his picture. At that point, one of the deputies asked Julie if she would like to see the rest of the jail. She went with the deputy and while they were gone, a few angry words were exchanged, then "thumps", "bangs", "bams" and they were then able to finish the booking process. He was charged with intoxication, disturbance and resisting arrest. On the way back to jail, Julie said, "if he had just kept his mouth shut he would not have had any problems". I told her, "People put themselves in jail, just with their mouths."

My dear wife, on a couple of occasions, had "some thing" for me. One midnight shift, I got a call of an ex-boyfriend refusing to leave. When I got to the location, I asked the young man, "Why don't you leave, she doesn't want to see you?" He said, "I just wanted to get back together with her." I asked him where his car was and he said he didn't drive because he had been drinking. I asked, "How did you get here?" He told me a lady cop had dropped him off. (From the typist – what the dirt bag said next was not true – not what he said to me….) I told her about my ex and she and told me she would take me to see her. I then told him, OK you have a big choice – you can go to jail for intoxication or I will put you in my car and take you back where you just came from. He decided and said he'd go back with me and I dropped him off on Barb's district. On our way home I asked her why she brought him to my district? She told me she felt sorry for him…(which I did as he had told me he had been drinking and shouldn't drive. He had a long walk home, so as was possible I gave his a "courtesy transport".)

Another night, Barb was attempting to pull a car over and radioed for assistance. I was sent and as I arrived, the car she was following, with lights and siren, pulled into a driveway. The driver got out, telling her, "I'm in my driveway, you can't arrest me. What are you going to do now"? She told him, "Well if I don't, he will" as she turned and pointed her finger at me. He went to jail with her for drunk driving.

Another snowy night, we both were sent to a residential alarm. I arrived first and found the home secure with no problems. I had called an immediate cancellation to stop other units and at the point saw Barb running up on foot. I asked her about not hearing the cancellation and she told me she heard it but needed my help. She had taken the corner too fast and slid up into a front yard and high centered onto an ornate area of the yard. I pushed her off and down the rise – there was no damage to vehicle or "yard". We quickly and quietly left the area…………………

One night I was dispatched to a disturbance at a residence with another one-man unit. I was first at the location and could hear the arguing as I walked up to the house. Once inside, I was able to get them to quiet down. I told them that one of them should leave, and asked, "Who wants to go?" I told them they needed to make up their minds. The husband said he would go. As I was starting to leave, the two started up again. I told them, "Go now, you are keeping your neighbors and me awake. If I have to come back again, both of you are going to jail! Again, I was on my way to my car and they both started yelling. I called dispatch and told him to send me a wagon as I had two arrests for disturbance. Yes, they both went to jail – I kept my promise to them.

AFTERNOONS

In June I took a report of a hold-up at a small carry-out (aka convenience store, stop and shop – many areas call them by different names). A black male entered the store, pointed a gun at the clerk, telling her, "This is a hold-up, give me all your money." He told her again, "I told you, this is a hold-up, give me all your fucking money." She gave him what was in the cash register. The suspect fled in an unknown direction with an undetermined amount of money. I notified 212 and broadcast the physical description of the suspect. A detective came to the scene for follow-up and I filed my report.

One afternoon there was a large disturbance at the Miracle Mile Shopping Center. Barb, her partner U-81, and I were dispatched. When we arrived the people who had caused the problem had left. While the three of us were talking, we were sent to a hold-up alarm at a bank. You had to be there to see the three of us taking off, lights and sirens, all in a row – one – two – three. We all arrived at the same time and found it was a false alarm. I still laugh when I think of what we looked like. A few, fun times - now and then.

I had a couple of calls with our K-9 Units. One day I was talking with one of the units, when we got sent to a silent alarm at a closed pizza restaurant. We were only a couple blocks away. We did not use our lights or sirens. We pulled up to the side of the restaurant, and then went to the front on foot. Looking inside the window, we observed a white male behind the bar and he was going through the cash register. Just then another unit arrived, with its red lights going. The suspect looked up and saw the reflection of the lights. He ran from the bar. We told the other crew to go to the rear to make sure he did not escape. The owner arrived and opened the door for us. Once inside, we found the basement door open. We yelled down to the suspect, "Come up with your hands up." No answer. The K-9 officer then said, "Come up now, or I'll send my dog down to get you!" He had his dog give a couple barks. We heard a voice from the basement, "Shoot me but don't send the dog down." When the suspect came up, we smelled something coming from him. He had crapped in his pants. More than likely it was because he was scared of the dog. We called for a wagon to transport him to 212. Aah, do you believe I was going to take him in the back of my car, nope, no way, now how. Felt sorry for the wagon crew and 212 but not that sorry.

It was busy that month. I had another call for a silent alarm at a sporting goods store. Once we got inside, the K-9 officer let his dog loose to locate the suspect. It was not a very long time before we heard the dog barking. The suspect was a black male and he was attempting to hide. Somehow he had gotten up into the "cold air return duct" for the furnace. Because of his weight, the duct had collapsed and was at an angle from the ceiling to the floor. The suspect was attempting to climb up but he kept sliding back down. Well, each time the slid down, the dog bit him in the butt. After stopping the dog and getting the suspect cuffed, he was arrested and transported to 212. Report was made.

In October '83 I worked a special duty after my regular shift. I worked at the Sheraton Hotel where, then Vice President George Bush, was staying. He was doing a fundraiser for the upcoming presidential elections. I was assigned to guard a locked door in a large empty room. As I was doing my guarding of a locked door in a large empty room – the other door opened and the Vice-

President walks in with all his people. He looks over at me, leaves everyone, and walks to me. He put his hand out to shake mine and says, "Officer how the hell are you?" I told him "Fine Sir". As he leaves, he tells me to have a good day. Hey, that was darn nice of him to acknowledge me.

One weekend morning, Barb and I were sent to an alarm at the florist in the Miracle Mile Shopping Center. The building was secure so we just talked while we waited for the owner to unlock the door. Once we were done checking the inside of the business we left. As I got back to my car, I found a large bunch of dead roses (typist – they were not dead just a little wilted.) on my front seat. I knew the only person that would or could do it was my wife. I asked her later about putting dead roses in the car and she told me "they weren't all dead and I did it because I love you." That's my wife.

As an afterthought, at the beginning of '83 I got another badge. I turned in Badge #232 and my new number was #50. Man did I jump up in seniority that time. The same month Barb and I were assigned to do traffic all day at an exit ramp on Interstate-75. During the night a propane tanker had over turned while attempting to use the exit. We were assigned to keep all traffic and people away from the area until another tanker could transfer the propane. Even with all the barricades and police cars, driver still tried to go around us. What gets into the minds of people – it was obvious this was a serious situation.

During this period of time, Barb and I were asked to work off duty at our church to guard the money. There had been several church robberies, which occurred just after the Sunday collections. The churches wanted armed guards and we helped our church about 6 or 7 times for about 6 months. That was part of our fun together because many of the projects (off duty work) allowed us to do it together. <u>A family that guards together stays together.</u>

On U-182 we had a lot of complaints from people living on Harvest Lane about drivers running a stop sign at one of the intersections. So whenever I had a few minutes to spare, I would set-up where I could watch the location. Yes, they did run the stop sign. Probably the best one I had was, when a vehicle had stopped for the sign, another car came up behind him…. drove to the left of the stopped car. He passed him at a high rate of speed and ran the stop sign. I took off after him, and caught up with the car at Monroe Street. I could have given him three citations – stop sign, passing at an intersection and speed. Each citation would have been (2) points on his license for a total of 6. Being a nice guy, I only gave him one citation – that being Operating without Due Regard – which gave him <u>6 points.</u> In Ohio, at that time, 12 points over a certain period would suspend your driving privileges. Your driver's license is only a "privilege" not a right and you need to remember that – drive safely and sanely.

May of '83, my times with Barb on the streets came to an end. She was being re-assigned back to the Detective Bureau, and not back to Juvenile. She became the first woman to be assigned to Adult Investigations and started in the Burglary Squad. This was a beginning not just for women on the department but it would bring about quite a few new adventures for the Palicki's.

CHAPTER SEVENTEEN

It will take a while for me to get used to going to work alone with Barb being assigned to the Detective Bureau. I became very spoiled having her with me, but I'll worry a little less with her in plain clothes.

AFTERNOONS – JUNE 1983

Barb and I had our first anniversary in Lake Tahoe. I had been there before but this was her first trip. She loved the place along with her newfound enjoyment – gambling. We would make more trips there in the future. It is still one of the most beautiful places to see. While there we visited an old friends, Tom and Jane Gradowski. I've known Tom since second grade. They were living in Sacramento and this was a chance to introduce them to Barb.

Sometime earlier I had put in for training to work the accident investigation unit. They handle all of the fatal and major injury accidents. The unit was also assigned any accidents involving city vehicles. I was assigned to work Unit-97, on and off, for the next few months. It was something different to try.

As I was waiting to hit-off one evening, I was sent to a criminal damage call with the suspect being held at the scene. When I arrived, I saw a vehicle setting in a front yard, with a crowbar sticking up in the hood. As I went to see what had happened, the owner of the property came up and said, "That kid was doing wheelies on my yard. I came out and hit his car with the crowbar a couple of times. I then stuck it in the hood." I questioned the young driver, "Why did you do that?" He did not answer me. I asked if he knew the man whose yard he tore up, and he said no. The homeowner did not know the driver either. I cited the young man for operating without due regard on private property and added a criminal damage charge. I told the driver that, "If you want to charge the man for damaging your car, a report will be made." I was off for the next two days and upon returning to work, I went back to the house to see the homeowner. I asked him if the young man had given him any more trouble. He told me, "No, in fact the boy and his father came back to see me." His father told me that his son is going to tell you he is sorry and he is going to do all the repair work to your yard himself. No one is going to help him and he will be using his own money to do it. If he hasn't enough he will just have to earn it. He will also be fixing his own car. Now that father is one great parent!

Another afternoon I got a call about a reckless driver on a residential street. When I got there a few upset neighbors told me that a certain person was on his motorcycle and using it as a hot-rod. They were able to get his license number. He had told the neighbors that he wasn't doing any thing wrong. They showed me various skid marks on the street. I ran a check on the plate number and it came back to the next street over. I drove to the suspect's house and as I was approaching, I heard a loud sounding cycle coming my way.

I waited for him and got him stopped. I questioned him about the people who had complained about his driving and he did say that he was on that street plus others. I cited him for excessive noise. I told the young man that if there were any more calls he would be cited into court and all the neighbors were more than willing to talk to the judge. Yup, remembered doing that back on U-16 and again it worked, no other calls came in concerning the motorcycle.

DAYS

One Sunday, my unit was pulled and I was assigned to work on Unit 152, the southwest part of the city. The one real interesting call I had was a disturbance at a home. My partner Unit 151 told me when we arrived that he had been there many times before. He said, "Wait until you see who it is and what he does." We could hear the occupants yelling at each other as we approached. We knocked and a man opened the door. Oh yes, I did know him (not personally) and what he had been – a retired judge. We finally got them to quiet down after a few minutes. He told us to come with him, stating, "I want to show you something." He took us to the bedroom. My partner nudged me as we went into the room. The man's wife was yelling for him not to take us there. He opens a dresser drawer, pulls out a handful of dildos and says, "See this is what she uses." Well…ok but what now? We got them calmed down again. We were able to get the man to leave and the problem seemed resolved for the time being. My partner said, "I told you it would be different". The call "made my day!"

One of the days I was assigned to the traffic U-97, I had a real bad one. It happened in the downtown area. A loaded dump truck was headed north on Erie Street at the intersection with Jefferson. He was in the west curb lane with a convertible in the lane to his right, next to him. The convertible, at the intersection, made a sharp left turn in front of the dump truck. The driver of the dump truck swerved to his left to avoid the convertible. As he swerved his load of gravel shifted causing the truck to turnover on its right side. The truck fell on top of the convertible and the driver of the car was totally covered in gravel and crushed to death. All the witnesses, that I interviewed, said about the same thing as to how the accident happened. You can imagine the length and amount of reports that needed to be done for such an incident.

One morning, after hitting-on, I was sent to a "Rape Call". The woman was at her home. She reported to me that she had met a man at a bar. After a while, they both left and ended up at his apartment. He started to kiss her, and she told him, "no". He then threw her on a bed and stripped off her clothes. She continued, stating, "I just lay there doing nothing. I did start to yell but he turned the radio up louder. He then raped me. He turned me over and then he anally raped me. He told me to pretend to enjoy it. You can have more if you want it. See, it wasn't so bad". She told me that when the man fell asleep she got dressed and left. I asked her, "Where did this happen?" She told me she didn't really know. She said she had just run away. I asked her what bar she had met him in and she told me she was not sure. I notified 212 and a detective came out to follow-up. Made another report.

NIGHTS

The middle of one night, Unit 191 and I were sent to a very loud disturbance on Douglas Road. It just so happened that the officer filling in on 191 was the same officer I had worked with when working 152. We heard yelling as we approached the door. A male answered the door and we asked, "Who called?" He stated that he did. He told us that he had gotten home from work early to be with his new girlfriend. He described that when he came in to the house, he found her in bed with another man. We asked where the other man was and the resident said, "He's gone". He called for his girlfriend to come out of the bedroom. We observed, as she came into the room, she was wearing only a very short, cut-off T-Shirt barely covering her "breasts". That was it -that was all she had on.... The male started screaming at her. We got him to quiet down and asked one of them to leave. The female said she would leave.

As she turned around, to go back into the bedroom, my partner said, "Look at her butt." Between the cheeks of her butt, there was a "turd" sticking out!!! We both started to laugh and could not stop laughing. As I'm writing this book, I still can't keep from laughing. As I hope you begin to see, working as a cop can be dull, very routine, some actions and then there are people and people can do bizarre things.

One Saturday night, my partner U-181 and I were sent to another large disturbance at a Wedding Reception. It was close to the end and some people were fighting. As usual the cause was too much drinking. While trying to get things calmed down, the groom came up to me and shoved me – the really wrong thing to do. We ended up on the floor. I was able to get him subdued and cuffed. Just then someone else jumped me from the side. I was able to get him by the neck, while sitting on the groom. While this was going on, my partner had also been jumped. He was able to call for help on the portable radio after getting his man cuffed. It seemed like an eternity before help arrived. Once they came in they ended up having to make more arrests. I think a total of five or six "partiers" went to jail. My two were charged with intoxication, assault and resisting. That was one hell of a way to start off a marriage – remember my first guy was the GROOM. His wedding night would be spent in a jail cell.

December 18, 1983 is my last time to work on nights. I'm on vacation for two weeks and when coming back in January, I will be on permanent "days". The department finally decided to go to permanent shifts. No more changing shifts every month. I can now sleep like a human being again!!! I had been working the swing shifts for almost 21 years. This is also my last night to work U-182. I had been in that district 10 years.

CHAPTER EIGHTEEN

JANUARY 1984 DAYS, DAYS, OH PERMANENT DAYS…

I did not bid on any specific crews or districts. I wanted to see what turned up or might come open. For the first couple weeks, I filled in all over where I was needed on the different crews or districts. After a short time, the department started a new Warrants Unit. All you did was look for persons wanted on outstanding warrants. The part that I didn't like was that we started at 3:00 to 4:00 am. We started out serving quite a few warrants. One in particular comes to mind. We were at a residence looking for a "John Jones". Not being able to locate him, we asked a young child, about 4 or 5 years old, "Do you like to play games?" He said yes. We asked if he liked "hide and seek" and he answered yes. We asked him, "Do you know where John Jones is hiding?" The little one pointed at a closet. We opened the door and all we observed was a large pile of clothes on the floor. The child kept pointing at the clothes. Well, guess who was under the clothes – Mr. Jones. Thanks Kid!!

After several months, I asked to be taken off the Warrants Unit. I just did not like getting up so early to go into work. I was put on a walking beat, like old times again. I walked mostly around the Portside area. I'd sometimes meet Barb for lunch at one of the restaurants at Portside. I filled in one day on Unit 81, which is in the northwest side of town. Someone had called saying that an airplane had landed in the parking lot at the Northgate Shopping Center. Sure enough, a small single engine plane was setting there. I asked the pilot what happened and he told me that it was an emergency landing. He said an oil line had broken. He said he was attempting to get parts to repair the problem. He made a great landing – no damage and no one injured. The plane was able to take off that day.

In March, I was assigned to work Units 71 and 9. Unit 71 was a Wagon and Unit 9 was a car. We were a relief crew. I worked with various partners in April. I was assigned a young African American Officer Varris. He was very likeable and I enjoyed showing him the ropes. That month, I found out that the Traffic Section had openings and the bid process was starting. I put in for it.

May 1984 I was taken off 71 & 9, being again a fill-in officer. I had no problems with that and actually spent most of my time on Unit 191, which was next to my old unit. It was like old home week. Until winter, I was a fill-in and did do a few beats downtown and a few times in dispatch.

November 1984 received a call from the Traffic Section telling me that I started the next day. They did ask if I still wanted it and I told them yes. That was my last day working on the street as a street officer. I did enjoy all those years, all the experiences, good and bad people I met and enjoyed all my partners. They are still my partners and friends.

CHAPTER NINETEEN

November 23, 1984 is my first day on the new job in the Traffic Section. I'll be working days, Monday to Friday, 7:30 am to 3:30 pm. We do however work one Saturday every seven or eight weeks. I'll now be known as Unit 555. To start out, I'll be working the "Hit-Skip" office and also learning to work the radar units. I've never been one to use or care about radar. For now through, I'll have to get use to doing it because it is part of the job. I told myself that I would always be fair. Considering that I do tend to have somewhat of a "heavy foot" myself. I normally will give a bit of leeway to drivers – 15 mph on the expressways – 10-12 on other streets and 5 mph in school zones. Kids are so important and it is possible that a person's speed-o-meter can be off.

Hit-Skip sounded interesting and it involves investigation. Driver's would come in and attempt to explain why their vehicles were involved in accident and how they “weren’t” driving, of course. After time I will have heard many lame and bizarre excuses.

The radar training involved 8 hours instruction by a qualified instructor and then 24 hours out on my own, observing cars, looking at the radar, and learning to judge, which was the speeder, when they were not the only car on the road. After all that, wow I can now give tickets. There was no quota – just two an hour – isn’t that a quota. The Traffic Section works on its own radio channel however dispatch monitored on channels on the chance that one of us called for help. Dispatch covered 5 channels – Traffic& Records, 212, 257, North Toledo and South Toledo.

One of the days in the Hit-Skip office, a driver came in after he received one of our “you need to appear letters” to tell us why he had left the scene of an accident involving his vehicle. He naturally denied being involved. Looking at the original report, I asked him, “Do you have damage to your vehicle and if yes, where on your car?” He stated, “Yes, it is on the left side of the car. It happened when a car hit me in a parking lot.” I asked him why he didn’t report it and he told me the car that hit him was gone and there wasn’t much damage. I said, “Ok, let’s go look at your car.” He told me he didn’t bring it. I then began calling the victim driver who was not home and left a message. I called the witness, and no one answered, but I continued and pretended to be talking to that person. I ask the ringing phone, can you tell me what happened and what you saw? During this time I’m looking at the suspect. I continue asking questions, “What did the driver look like and what was he wearing?” Oh, you say he had black hair with gray in it and he was wearing a ball cap. Ok and you say he had a small matching color beard. I continued to describe the suspect's car and said the "license plate". I told the ringing phone, that I appreciated his help and he would be contacted if he were needed for court.

I then looked the suspect in the eyes, and asked, "Are you still telling me that you were not at the accident?" "Yah, ok, I was the driver and I left because I don't have any insurance!!" I explained, "Sir, if you had come in and told the truth to begin with you would have only gotten one or two citations, but now you are getting one for the accident, one for leaving the scene, one for no insurance, and one for having an expired driver's license. That was fun to con him into an admission. That is one of the fun parts of the job.

Any time there was a big snowstorm, accidents increased drastically. The street officers were not able to take them all. If there were no injuries or intoxicated driver involved, they would be advised to come to the Traffic Section to make a report. It was extremely hectic during those times, lines of people and lots of reports.

In January 1985 I was told to assist one of my fellow officers, J. Lee, in Traffic. He was assigned to the Junk Auto Squad. The department had approximately 12 tow yards that towed for us. The vehicles would be towed for many reasons, and after 30 days, Officer Lee would go to the yards, checked each vehicle to determine which would be junked and which would be saved for the Police Auction. I was to learn his job so I could fill in for him during vacations or other days he was away.

This training day with him was extremely cold and as you would know, tow yards are in the open. We were at one on Laskey Road and had a dozen or so cars to check. We were required to take pictures of all cars that were to be junked. Our camera (in those days) was a Polaroid and because it was so cold, we could not take pictures. We finally put it on a heater to warm it up and then ran, yup literally ran, to the car and took a picture, then ran back to the office area to see if it would develop. If not, we had to do it again. As you could imagine what normally would have only been an hour to hour and a half, took us all day just to work one lot. Remember Toledo, Ohio has real winters and below 0 chill factors.

Little did I know that day, that not too far down the road, I would be working that position until I retired?

CHAPTER TWENTY

After returning from a short vacation in Las Vegas, early in 1984, one of the kids told Barb that some Deputy Chief from the police department called and wanted her to call as soon as she got back. Barb called in and he wanted to meet her at a local park but not to tell anyone on the department. She did not tell me anything at that time. When she came back home she told me that the department wanted her to run an undercover sting operation. She added that it depended on me being agreeable to the idea and allowing her to do it. They wanted me to know that for much of the time she would be alone however there would be a hidden video recorder while at the location taping continuously.

After we talked it over, I agreed, as there really was no way to say "no" to this opportunity in her career. The operation lasted approximately seven months and they made about 120 arrests at the end in October. Part of the sting was a "con" to explain where she was. The officers were told that she was temporarily assigned to the Law

Department across the street to "investigate sexual harassment cases". She had to appear at the police department and be seen picking up her paycheck. The sting was a store in east Toledo and was named Bobby Peels Used Goods. It was literally named for the man who founded the "Bobbies" in England. During the seven months there was another undercover drug officer who spent most of his time in the street buying drugs and helping to pass the word that "Bobby" liked to buy things. (Bobby had many experiences during that time and maybe will write that in her book, after she gets this one done.) We bought drugs, weapons, and most anything that could be stolen and fenced.

Our neighbors never knew what she was doing or what she was driving. She was issued a brown camero, fairly new. We would leave the garage door open and she would pull in at night and close it. She would then get out of her wig and clothes. Mornings she could get into the car and drove out with no one seeing her or if they did, recognizing her.

I always did my best to stay away from her "store" though it was a temptation to make sure she was all right. One day, late afternoon, Barb calls home and says her undercover car has a dead battery. She couldn't call the "city tow" to come jump-start the car. Doug and I went to the store and worked fast hoping no one would pull in and see us, or if they did maybe they'd think we were just a couple of her cronies.

I keep bugging her about writing her own book because being woman she had to always prove herself during her career, more so then a man would. She was always questioned even when she proved she could handle the job and herself. This was both in Ohio and then in

Oregon where she ended up retiring after 34 years in law enforcement.

Around May of 1985, the City of Toledo passed a Nuisance Abatement Act, which gave us the right to remove any “junk auto” within the city limits. I was assigned to this unit permanently. This turned out to be the best job I ever had, and worked Junk Auto until retiring in 1994. We had the whole city to work. Initially Officer Lee and I were the only ones in the unit, though later, due to the work load two additional officers were assigned.

When a complaint of a “junk” was called in, we would go out and locate the complainant. It might be the property owner or the vehicle owner. The person would sign a form permitting us to remove the vehicle at no charge. If the person refused to allow a “free removal”, then they were given 3 days to either remove it themselves or show us that it started and could move. If the time came and went with no resolution, we would make a report, stating what we had done to attempt to alleviate the problem and would have pictures showing the condition of the “junk”. We would then submit the information to the abatement committee and wait for authorization to remove the vehicle.

The first 6 months we averaged 200 cars a month and this did not count the ones that Officer Lee junked at the tow yards. I had known we had a lot of junks in the city but never imagined how many there really were. A few were decent enough to hold for the auction but most of them were useless.

Talk about the different excuses we got when talking to people about their “vehicle”. We normally would ask whose car is it and does it run? They'd answer, what junk? Oh that car runs! Ok, start it! The answer would be, "Oh well it won't start now, it needs a transmission, part of the motor is gone, it needs a drive shaft, a radiator, or just a total overhaul. These were just a few of the answers. Sir, that's fine but you have 3 days to get it moved or working. I'll be back.

I had a call to check out a car in an alley. It was an old "T-Bird". Picture this and you will realize just how long that car had been in one place. Growing through the driver's window and out the passenger's window was a "tree branch". I found the owner of the T-Bird. He was given his choice and told that since it was Friday, he had until Monday to move it. The first place I went Monday was the alley and had a tow truck with me. Lo and behold, the bird was gone and all that was left was the sawed off tree limb. No fun of a tow but it accomplished what was needed.

Another classic involved a vehicle that had sat long enough to allow "weeds" to grow up and out of the carburetor. It would have been interesting to know how long it took for the weeds to grow. That classic was a tow and junk.

One Friday, I get a call about a VW sitting in the driveway of a vacant house. I was able to locate the owner of said bug next door. He was told that he had 3 days to get it moved because the owner of the property wanted it moved and would sign the order. Being a nice guy, again, I gave him until Monday. Of course, I got the usual, "Ok it will be moved". Returned Monday and the car was still there. I called for the tow and attempted to get the car owner to respond to his door. Ah, but then as soon as the truck came and was hooked up to the car, out runs the owner and wanted to remove some tools and items from the car. I told him, "Ok go ahead". What happened next was hysterical; you just really needed to be there. He opens the driver's door and jumps in landing very hard on the seat. I heard a loud, "Ahhhh". All I see is the top of his head. The seat had literally gone through the floorboards and he was now sitting on the driveway. Though it was funny then, think about him driving this vehicle on a city street and having that happen and possibly causing an accident.

I wish I would have thought fast enough to take a picture, could have made some money. In those days, police cars did not have in-car video recorders. One other thing we learned in the Junk Auto Unit was to make lots of noise by hitting the vehicle, you'd be surprised how many rats, mice, and other vermin would run away. We always wore gloves when we had to go through and search these treasures. We were required to search thoroughly for any items of value. If we seized anything it had to be logged into the property room.

I never did find any large sums of money. We did find weapons, of all types, and one in particular, was a 9mm Sig Sauer, belonging to one of our own officers. It had been taken during a burglary at his home. I found it hidden down a fender well, inside the trunk. Also came across a variety of "sex toys". Located many tools, chainsaws, and of course, rats and vermin.

CHAPTER TWENTY-ONE

On September 22, 1985 our son, Mike, is appointed to the Toledo Police Department. He will be attending the academy for the next five months. When he had signed up to take the test, he was given a study manual. Barb and I would look in the book and make up tests for him to take. He must have worked as he was hired.

There are now (3) officers named Palicki. While there were many fathers and sons, and soon "daughters", this was a first "family" for Toledo Police. Law enforcement can run generations through many families. At that time, my brother-in-law, from the first marriage, Detective R. Ruppi, was also working on the department.

Because of the heavy amount of complaints we were getting on junk cars and that many times we were unable to locate either the property or vehicle owner, we came up with a new plan. We set up a meeting with the City Health and Inspection Division and they would sign the forms for us, allowing us to remove the vehicles in question. They were easily determined to be health and safety hazards. Bingo – we had a new way to remove the vehicles in questions. Oh most certainly they were hazards with all the rats, mice and other vermin in and around them. Also they were heavily damaged with glass and metal causing safety issues. They also were a convenient place to throw trash. We made many people happy and then, of course, we made many people not so happy, but so be it.

February 7, 1986 Mike graduated from the police academy. His first day on the job was February 10th. Good luck son – hope you have a safe and great career on the department.

We got our first order from the Nuisance Abatement Committee allowing us to remove the vehicles that the owners, did not remove or refused to remove, the posted vehicle after being told to do so. We were still required to post them again and would be back in three days to get them. The order to remove those vehicles was a large one (quite a lengthy list) rather than issuing one or two at a time.

Officer J. Lee and I spent a couple days towing those vehicles. We worked together just in case we would have problems (trouble). One of the first we towed and junked was an old, rusty VW Station Wagon. When the tow driver hooked it up and started to lift it, the wagon split in two. He had to call for a flatbed truck to come and take the pieces. While we were doing this, the owner of the vehicle called the police department to complain that his car was being "stolen" by us. A detective from the Auto Squad was dispatched and we explained to him the process and that it was a new program that the city had implemented to rid the city of these "eye-sores". The detective told us, "Sound Great, Bye!"

In July 1986, I threw myself a "two-day 50th Birthday party". I had made it to the half-century mark. On Saturday, I invited all my ex-partners and people I now worked with including their wives or significant others. The next day, Sunday, I had all my relatives and friends over. We went through a keg of beer each day. I made most of all the food. Barb made her "infamous" baked beans, salad and other items. It was quite a two-day party.

In the fall of 1986, the Health and Inspection Division had been trying to get a "junk yard" on the east side to clean up their property. The junkyard, for whatever reason, refused to do as asked. We helped the city department remove all the vehicles on the property. It was at this time that another officer was added to our squad. Officer Orze. The three of us were there for two full days. We took over 70 to 75 vehicles from the location. Each one had to be checked, valuables removed, photograph taken and VIN number run to make sure it was not a stolen vehicle. Each vehicle required a report.
It was a down and dirty job. The city even issued us coveralls on the "last day". As you all know, junkyards are just plain dirty. Is it worth it? Yes. Is it a glamorous "cop" job? No. It involves exactly what you swear to do that first day – To Serve and Protect….

Making your city safe and free of blight. No glamour – no "TV Cops Show", you serve your community.

TOLEDO
POLICE
TOLEDO
POLICE

CHAPTER TWENTY-TWO

October 1, 1986, just finishing my daily tow paperwork, I was suddenly in pain. My kidney stones, again. Officer Orze rushed me to the hospital. The doctors there asked me, "Are you sure it's a kidney stone?" After I told them what type of pain I was having, they agreed. I told them I know the pain well. I was off work until the 13th. After the stones were removed, they asked me if I wanted them. "Hell, No"... I did tell people that I gave birth to triplets (had three stones).

"Typist Note: Of course I was called in the Bureau and got to the hospital. Stayed and then just after his surgery, I went in and being the loving wife – I sat down on the "bed" to give him comfort. Poor baby! I was chatting away and then realized he wasn't talking and I looked at him. His eyes were very large and he kept pointing. I looked down and realized I was sitting on the catheter tubing and it was "pulling" it out – oops".

July 8, 1987, Vice-President George Bush came back to Toledo for a political rally. This time I was assigned to downtown Traffic while he was in town. He didn't have a chance to say high to me this time, oh well his loss.

Later in 1987 I found a stripped and banged up vehicle in an alley behind a vacant house. I ran a check on it using the VIN as the plates were missing. I was told it was a "clean car", not stolen. I ordered a tow to junk it. It had to be put on a flatbed truck. A short time later I was notified that the car was stolen out of Detroit, Michigan. I went to the junkyard, after telling dispatch to call the yard to let them know that it was stolen and not to "junk it". When I arrived the vehicle was in the air above the "crusher". Thank God, it was still there. Of course, another report and we had to call a regular tow to take it to their yard. After that I never heard what happened but a detective would have to be assigned to decide what to do.

Some time later, I had another stolen auto that I was going to junk. This one was totally stripped out. It was nothing but an empty shell. I was able to find the VIN and when I called for a tow and gave the number, records advised someone was "just reporting it stolen". Apparently the owners had just come home from an extended vacation and the Buick they were restoring was not in the garage. The owners came to the location and they took one look at what was left and both started to cry.

This year, I had a slight change of assignment for a couple weeks. I had to work with the "Sign Shop". My assignment was to lead a paint truck on the city streets so they could paint the white and yellow traffic lines. Not a bad duty – just different.

On one of the Saturdays that I had to work in the traffic office, I was taking a statement to add to an original traffic accident report. One of the drivers involved brought in a witness to the accident in an attempt to change what had occurred. This driver had been cited for the accident at the scene. This witness had "suddenly" made himself known to this driver. While talking to the "witness", I asked him for his ID. He gave me his driver's license and I ran a check on him, guess what? The witness was wanted on an outstanding warrant. I asked the driver who had brought in this "witness", if she still wanted to change his story about the accident?"

As we were waiting for someone to take the "witness" to jail, he told me he did not see the accident and only wanted to help her (the driver) out of a ticket. The lady driver looked at me and used a couple curse words, turned away and left the office. I added what had happened to the original report. The non-serious accidents can be so much fun and hearing the stories and what drivers will do to get out of their situation.

CHAPTER TWENTY-THREE

Sometime around the start of 1988, Officer Lee Besse and I started to share the same police car. If you remember, Lee called me later in the day after we had Kathy's funeral. I used the car on day shift and he used it on the 8 pm to 4 am "special high crime" shift. We made a deal that I would keep it clean for us and make sure to turn it in whenever maintenance was needed. He agreed to keep it waxed and help to keep it clean inside and out. The city had a contract with a Car Wash at Front and Main, on the east side of Toledo. One flat rate and they washed the city cars with no limit on how many washes. One morning I was getting in the car and I slid across the seat and my feet slid also. Lee had used "Armorall" on the whole interior of the police car.

Trust me – I mean everything. I saw him later that day, as he was one of our neighbors only 4 houses down. I told him, "don't ever do that again, you almost killed me!" He told me, "Ok, I just won't use as much next time". We did have the cleanest police car in the city fleet. Every so often we were both off at the same time and other officers would use the car. Of course, it would be dirty when we got it back. Both of us wanted a clean car as we considered it our "office". One day when we knew we were both off, Lee put a "steering wheel lock" on the car. You should have heard the "bitching".

We told them they also could have clean cars if they took care of them. The city could not always replace cars that often and you wanted to keep them in good shape, especially inside. You live in your car for a minimum of 8 hours.

A very sad day – 1-17-88 – My old partner and friend, Doug Baden, was buried. Doug had resigned a few years before to start his own business. Late one evening he had slipped on some ice and fell. He struck his head on a cement step and when he was found he was dead. My other partner, from our days on Unit-16, Detective Bob Bannon and I attended his funeral. So long partner and friend!

April 18, 1988, guess who came to town today? President George Bush. We were assigned to escort him from the Toledo Express Airport to downtown Toledo and back. This was a new assignment – we had to learn to "leapfrog" from one entrance ramp to the other, making sure no one entered until his caravan had passed. All I can say is the caravan was going a little over the speed limit. As we, had our cars to the floor board, just to keep up and be able to pass to get to the next entrance ramp.

From mid-1988, I started from then until the time if my retirement, to take advantage of making extra cash which would add to my retirement package. Every Memorial Day weekend and also Labor Day weekend, the city had hydroplane boat races on the Maumee River. This went on for three or four years and allowed me to not only make extra money but to have a good "vantage point" to watch the races.

One of the weekends, the crane operator, who put the boats in and then pulled them out, had an accident. One of the straps that held a boat broke and the boat fell. The boat landed on another racing boat on the ground. It totaled both boats. We had to keep the peace as both boat owners want to do bodily harm to the crane operator. You could understand how they felt but it wasn't his fault. The strap broke.

On October 10, 1988, my old friend, President George Bush, came back again to attend a political event. I was assigned to the same traffic escort. I began to think that if this continued, George and I would have to start exchanging Christmas and Birthday cards.

On November 8, 1988 I was called in off the street. Barb got very sick at work and I rushed her to the hospital. She spent two nights there and had a very bad case of Bronchitis. I don't need scares like that anymore!!

Late December 1988, we had another junkyard to empty for the City Health and Inspection Division. This one was on Broadway in south Toledo. They would not comply with the order to "clean-up". A week before Christmas, the four of us (Junk Squad) went to the yard. We ended up junking over 400 vehicles of all types. Yes, everyone had to be checked out – one at a time. A private junking company was brought in with their own crusher. When we finished processing a vehicle, it was taken to the crusher. It took about 5 minutes to have a "flat car". This place was much dirtier that the one we did before, plus it was “cold”. We spent the week before Christmas freezing.

CHAPTER TWENTY-FOUR

FEBRUARY 1989

The department transitioned to a totally new radio communications system. Units were renumbered and instead of Unit 555, I became Unit-55. I was also issued a new hi-tech portable radio #097. The portable can be handheld or inserted into a sending/receiving unit in the car. The best feature of the new units was the emergency RED BUTTON.

When the button is hit, all radio traffic is stopped and dispatch begins attempting to locate the officer assigned to the radio. Once it is determined the officer is ok and it was an accidental hit, the system goes back to normal radio traffic. The feature was wonderful. Picture yourself working alone and getting into a fight with one or more subjects. You will tell even one to hold off so you can make a radio call – right! You normally can get your finger on the button…and help will be immediately on the way. There are other situations where it would be a lifesaver.

One day I stopped for a quick car wash and left the radio on the seat. As the car went through, an attendant had gotten in to wipe down the inside and moved the radio. He accidentally hit the button. I had no idea what was going on until I got back in the car and heard the dispatcher trying to get me and other officers searching. It was a little embarrassing as it tied up the radio for 10 minutes.

March 6, 1989 was another sad day. One of my fellow officers in Traffic died suddenly. He was not sick and just passed away over the weekend. Officer Rich "Rap" Brownne was one of the most likeable people I had ever known.

Midway through 1989, the department started a new program – weighing large trucks that went through Toledo on the city streets. The state already had a weigh program on the state highways and Toledo decided to do it also. There were two reasons for the program. One was the fact that overweight trucks can damage the roadways and two the money generated from fines could be utilized to maintain the streets.

Officer Lee, my junk partner, put in for the new position. Command asked if I wanted to replace him and cover all the junkyards, and of course, I said yes. Taking on the yards would leave me only one to one and a half days to do the regular "junks". It would still work out as they had two other officers assigned to junks.

It was about this time that I started to take advantage of working radar. The city would get special grants to set up on the expressways going through the city. They would run the program from Thursday through Saturday, usually from 8:00 pm to 2:00 am. I did it mainly to build up my "retirement". Did I say that word again – retirement? Have I been on that long to even be thinking retirement? Thinking back we were told in the Police Academy – "Before you know it, your time on the job will be over. You will many times be bored and think time "drags" but then one day you wake up and all those years have flown by…where does time go when you are having fun."

On our vacation out west in 1989, we thought we had found our retirement property in Brookings, Oregon. We were unable to come to terms with the owner. Oh well, that is how things go and we were going to try the next year. We had made up our minds that Brookings was the "retirement" home.

April 1990, Mike met and fell in love with a wonderful gal, Dawn. We both love her as a daughter and want their marriage to be full of love and long lasting. That year also, I began projecting (extra work) at the July 4th fireworks. I planned to do it every year until retirement. It is now held downtown rather that at Walbridge Park in south Toledo. It was quite an affair and involved a multitude of people. Officers always worked in pairs. I never had a problem but many other officers did at different times. As you would imagine, alcohol and drugs could play a large part in crowd behavior.

At the start of my vacation in 1990 I had another kidney stone, and it hit the second day of my time off, rats…. I thought I was through with them. It worked out though, as we did not have any out of town plans.

As a part of the radar on the highways, Ohio Highway Patrol would send an airplane at selected times of the year to patrol the expressways. We would then have four offices and a Sergeant assigned to the area. We would wait for the airplane to spot a speeder. He would then radio where the vehicle was, which way it was traveling. He would continue to track and once we got the vehicle pulled over, we would give him the make and license plate number. He would provide the speed and we would do this for about two hours. During that time we would get 6 to 8 citations per officer.

One I do remember quite well. As I was finishing a citation on a stop, the pilot came on the air and asked if any officer was near the split at I-75 and I-475. I told him that I was just finished and he advised that he had a brown car headed my way. He then said it is passing you now…. Just then a 2-door Brown Mustang literally flew by. I gave chase and caught him about a mile up the road. He was clocked at 90.

Another thing we did with Ohio Highway Patrol, several times, was catching drivers who drove around lowered railroad crossing gates. Toledo was surrounded with railroad crossings. We would have two cars stationed at a specific crossing. The state had a "special train" that would travel at a slow speed. A helicopter would be overhead following the train. We were positioned on the two sides of the crossing. If and when a vehicle would go around the gates, we would catch them. It was surprising how many idiot drivers would take that chance. Maybe we saved a life or two. They would always argue entrapment or hiding, but we didn't make them break the law.

We also would set up at intersections for the “Seat Belt Blitz”. We would walk up the line of cars that were stopped for the “red light” and check the driver and passengers for seat belt usage. During those, we would tell them to buckle-up and not issue a citation. If we found the car had all belts used – we would then give then a little gift from the state. We would thank them for being good drivers and passengers. It was a great PR program and hopefully it also saved a life or two.

During this year, Officer Lee and I had started to eat with the guys at “204”. 204 was the phone extension for the city garage. They took care of all the maintenance and repairs to the police vehicles. We made friends with one of the men, Rob. Whenever we would need “something special” done to our cars, Rob was the go to guy and he took care of us. He knew that we did not “abuse” our cars as so many others did.

Rob and some of his co-workers loved fish and a couple Fridays a month, we would have a fish fry with them. We would donate cash or bring what they needed. Some times it would be dessert or drinks (just soda pop!!). We all were working so nothing livelier could be consumed. They did an excellent job and the meals were darn good. No one went away hungry. Just remembering makes me hungry!

CHAPTER TWENTY-FIVE

MARCH 1991

Another new "police car", still using Chevrolet Caprices. Another one to keep in top shape and make the other crews envious. One thing I should have mentioned before about doing all the "junk yards"…making friends. I had decided that having to go on to the properties, I needed to make friends with the "junk yard dogs". Not all the yards had them but several did. They were there to keep "unwanted" guests away especially at night when folks like to help themselves to "parts". I always carried a large box of dog bones in the car. After a while, they all got to know me and as soon as the police car pulled in, here they came running. They would then follow me around, keeping me company, while I checked the cars.

I felt sorry for them being alone at night. No one to keep them company. It was not easy as several times I would show up and no one came to great me. I'd ask about where my friend was and would be told that over night or over a weekend someone had shot and killed my friend. What a bunch of worthless sick people. The same should be done to them!!

One friend was "Bear" and he looked the part. He was part Great Dane, the other parts – who knows? He was at one of the east Toledo yards and we became very good friends. One day as I was doing my paperwork in the yard's office, Bear came in. I told the owner, "Watch this!" I got a bone out, put it between my lips and he took it gently from my mouth. Bear ate the bone and then licked my face. The owner stated, "Nuts, don't do that, I'm trying to keep him "mean"." I just laughed, and told the owner, "Hey, he needs to know that some one cares about him and that's me, too bad."

Barb and I took another vacation out west to look for property and this time we found it. It was an acre of land with many trees. It was located about 5 1/2 miles up the South Bank of the Chetco River on Mt. Emily Road. We could see Mt. Emily from the property. We were told that about an hour drive from the property, further up the mountain, was the Bomb Site. During WWII, the Japanese bombed the forest in an attempt to start forest fires. It did not work because, unknowing to them, it was our rainy season. The area is what is known as a Rain Forest. A submarine equipped with a small airplane, in a special hangar on the deck, got close enough to the coast to have the plane take off. He flew to our area and dropped incendiary bombs. The plane flew back to the submarine and left. I have been to the site several times and take friends there whenever they visit.

Just as an insert side-note, while we have been here, the "Japanese pilot" of the plane that bombed Mt. Emily, visited several times and presented to Brookings his family's Samurai Sword, which is now displayed at the library. It was quite a ceremony and he since passed away and his ashes are at the Bomb Site. He was quite a guy – a regular soldier, like ours, who follow orders though maybe not too sure what it is all about.

Back in Toledo, the summer of 1991 the city started having "Party in the Park" along the riverfront downtown. They were held every Friday evening during the summer. They had various musical groups, vendor booths, and, of course, a beer tent. I had traffic at an intersection, helping people get in and out of the "party". I did this my last three years during the summers.

At the end of July 1991, our son, Doug, got married. Barb had a small reception for Doug and Angie at our home. We wished them the best as we had Mike and Dawn. At that time, Doug was seriously thinking about becoming a fire fighter for Toledo. He must have been serious as he signed up to take the test and we are helping him. Like Mike, Doug had a booklet to study from and we did question and answer sessions with him.

In October 1991, we had a very sad incident involving an off-duty officer. He had worked a neighboring district next to me when I worked U-182. His daughter was involved in a traffic crash. She called her father while at the scene to help her. He arrived at the crash and while standing there, a drunk driver slammed into him pinning him into another vehicle. He passed away several days later. Why do these things happen to the good guys?

November 1991 I assisted the Taxi Cab Inspector. We had to check out all the local taxicabs that operated within the city. We had to check the accuracy of the "meters". We would have the driver drive the cab over a measured course. About 10% of them were not even close to being accurate. We also check them for being able to stop, and graded them on cleanliness. We would actually stomp our feet on the floorboards to make sure they were solid. On several of them, we actually went through to the pavement. Quite a few cabs got "grounded" and had to re-test before they were allowed back on the road.

December 10 1991, another political escort – today the Vice President Dan Quale came to Toledo for a speech. It felt like old times and there were no serious problems.

Since Barb and I had made definite plans about the property and tentative retirement, she went to work on Afternoon in the Detective Bureau. This was to help increase her retirement. Afternoons in the Bureau were 3:00 pm to 11:00 pm. You worked anything that came in and assisted the uniformed officers with felony arrests. In most cases an arrest at night would be arraigned the next morning in court. This meant a lot of court overtime. She seemed to like it because you worked a variety of cases, what you were needed to help with.

CHAPTER TWENTY-SIX

APRIL 1992

Another "new badge", I traded badge #50 for BADGE #2, which will be my last badge. The reason I know is that the current officer wearing BADGE #1 is not planning on retiring any time soon and I will be gone before then. It is still awesome being number two in seniority.

About the middle of 1992, after traffic had a couple retirements and job assignment changes, I am now the only one left on junk autos. Oh well, as I had previously said most of my time is spent in the yards. What little time left will be used for the "street" complaints. There is nothing that can be done and production will drop drastically.

August 21, 1992 I had an all day special – it's election time again and the Vice-Presidential "Hopeful" Al Gore was in town. Again, good security and no problems, that is what you hope for when doing this job.

The next day, Saturday the 22nd, we did some thing new. In the evening from 9 pm to 3 am, we did a special "drunk driver checkpoint". It was set up on Alexis Road. We had to "advertise" it in the newspaper for a week and then on that day we had to advertise the exact location and time. "Our goal was to get drunk drivers off the road – why do we have to warn them?" Traffic cones were used to make the vehicles use only one lane on that section of road. We would then stop one out of four as they went through. The law required that even though the (3) in between were drunk, they could not be stopped.

My position was at the far end of the checkpoint. Any suspicious vehicle was radioed to me and I would stop them and check out the driver. I did get a couple of drunks, plus others who had suspended licenses and any other problems. There were twelve of us working at the checkpoint. It actually worked "so good" we ran out of other crews for transport. How did we get so many? The city had just purchased several new "portable handheld intoxilyzer" for instant testing.

We had one female driver, who was so drunk she did not even stop. She drove through all the cones and finally had to be stopped by blocking her with a police car. It was a very interesting night to say the least.

September 9, 1992, issued another new car – a 92 Chevy Caprice and a nice one to baby. September 24, 1992 and it was my turn to go to Sensitivity Training from 8 am to 4 pm. I still do not know if it was worth it or not. First thing that happened, I got into a disagreement with the trainers. How? Well, their idea was that when we introduced ourselves to the class, we were to also tell them where we came from – i.e. German-American, Irish-American, African-American or whatever. When it was time for me, I said that I am an American. I was told by a trainer, No, you are not – you are a Polish-American. I answered, "No, I am an American. I was born in this country, not another country. In fact, I am second generation born American." Back and forth it went – No, you're not, and then yes, I am". Finally I said, "what do you put on your "Passport" when you get one – born American". They were not happy with me and they graciously said I could leave – to which I answered, "No I can't – I was ordered here!" I was not bothered the rest of the day and at the end I did get my certificate of attendance. I still think I'm right!!!!!

October 2, 1992, another special assignment – some guy named "Clinton" who was running for President came to town. I did not do escort but did do traffic and guard the area.

October 17th we had another "Drunk Driver Checkpoint". It was set up for the same hours and this time we did it on Broadway in south Toledo. We did not get as many as the first time, but still got enough to make it more than worthwhile. This time I was assigned to the beginning of the area and it was not as exciting. The one part of a checkpoint is "you must post a sign and notify drivers one or two blocks before what is ahead. They must have a side street or two so they can divert and miss it". The game is really all on their side. Most though were so drunk, they couldn't read anyway.

CHAPTER TWENTY-SEVEN

APRIL 1993

On April 12, I had another special traffic and guard duty, this one for now Vice-President Al Gore. He was to appear at some function and would be in town only about 3 hours. No problems and an apparent success.

Also in April, and the next three months, we received a special grant. This one involved checking on people who had been convicted of two or more drunk driving charges. We worked this once a week for four hours at a time. We could choose when to work it from Monday to Friday. Hey, like I said, the extra money goes towards retirement. We would meet with the person and see how they were doing and if we could help in anyway. I was able to help one young man get his license back. I did have one guy that I never saw during the entire time. He was never home no matter what time I went. I did talk with his mother and she did tell me that he wasn't driving. She showed me his car, which was totally wrecked sitting in the garage. She did tell me that he "had not quit drinking". She described that he would go to the blood bank and sells his blood to get money to buy alcohol. I doubt that he ever was able to quit drinking.

We had about twelve people to check up on during the period of the grant. I had no problems with any of my assigned people. A few of them did not really care what was happening in their lives. What a life they led. It was sad but so be it, family and even the cops offered them help.

July 12, 1993 – I qualified at the range for the "last time". I shot 49 out of 50 – not bad for an "ole cop". This was also the last time to clean my Sig.

July 16, 1993, our son, Doug, was sworn in at the Toledo Fire Department. This now made it (4) with the last name of Palicki on the city payroll, not counting my brother-in-law Ruppi and his new son-in-law. Now six relatives on the payroll – if we kept it up we could "take over" the city.

August 14 and 15, we worked at a special at the Inverness Golf Club for the U.S. Open Tournament. It was a nice, easy assignment. I was assigned with another officer at the "Players Gate". We were there from 6:30 am to 8:00 pm both days. We got to know who was coming and going. The players and some VIPS provided good food and drinks at the post. Of course, again the drinks for us were only "soda pop".

September 30, 1993, time is getting close and this is my last time to wear a summer uniform. I'm down to months.

Also today, we had to turn in our last new car for another car, which was not new. It was the same year as ours however our car had far few miles on it. The city was trying to even out mileage on the different vehicles in the fleet. Your car is like a "friend" and while we were changing out the cars, I watched the new crew piling equipment and stuff on the hood – scratching and scraping it. It hurt to watch. Needless to say it did not take us long to bring the new "ole" car up to our standards. First trip was to the car wash and then we both worked on it –inside and out.

November 11, 1993, all the special grants have come to an end, as does our overtime. It will start again in 1994 but by then, I will be gone. On this same day, Doug graduated from the Fire Academy. We wish a safe and long career, though we know he will be great and leave a mark on the department.

December 31, 1993, my last full year on the Toledo Police Department – I am now down to only weeks to work.

CHAPTER TWENTY-EIGHT

Today, January 3, 1994, I am training my replacement, Officer Gary Thompson. He is the new junk auto man. During training, I'll be taking him to all the yards to introduce him to the owners and employees. He will also be shown how to get the junks removed from private property.

Something else coming to an end, it's my 25 years of "projecting" at the University of Toledo and having worked most of the time with my good friend, Gary Cooke. Hey, Gary we did have some good times working there, didn't we? But that would be another story, so long Gary!

January 25, 1994, is my last day on junks. Officer Thompson is now doing the yards. I towed my last junk off private property today. I met a couple of old partners for lunch today and it was kind of sad.

January 26, 1994, my last day in uniform. I got up this morning, went to the closet and looked at the uniforms – thinking, "This is it!" I loaded my gun for the last time, dressed for the last time and drove off to work! Today is the "good-bye" day. I met Detective Bannon for breakfast and then I went around to all the yards to say goodbye. I went around the Safety Building to others I had worked with for a last time.

When I got home, I unloaded the gun, took off my shirt, opened the hamper and tossed it in. I stood there thinking, "just tossed a dirty shirt in the hamper and a career and life style ends!" That quick and where did those years go?

The job has been good to me. I was able to do so many interesting things those years. I hope that I did a good job. I tried to treat everyone fairly. I had many happy times and too many sad times. I know that I will miss some of it – mostly the people that I have worked with, and the friends made along the way. BUT IT IS TIME FOR ME TO MOVE ON…

January 27th, 1994, this morning I have to turn in all my equipment – gun, badge #2, handcuff, and keys – It was a terribly empty feeling. After dropping the equipment off, I went to the Traffic Section – hugs the ladies, shook hands with the guys and yes, I had a tears in my eyes as I left for that last time.

Later that evening the Traffic Section threw me a retirement party and close to 80 people came. A wonderful gal from Traffic, who was a civilian employee, was the one responsible. Thank you, Chris Black. All, especially me, had a good time.

SO ENDS MY TIME AND LIFE ON THE TOLEDO POLICE DEPARTMENT AND WHAT WAITS FOR US IN OREGON?????????

PATROLMAN
RETIRED
TOLEDO
POLICE
OHIO
OHIO
2

Daniel J. Palicki
TOLEDO
04-01-63
01-27-94
POLICE
PROUDLY PRESENTED BY
TOLEDO POLICE
PATROLMAN'S ASSOCIATION

EPILOG

Reading back over the book, I found many things I had not mentioned. I will use this section to comment on those subjects.

Firstly, I need to tell you more about my beautiful wife, Kathy. Kathy wanted to be a dedicated mother, wife and homemaker for our family. Kathy quit working just before the birth of our second son, Doug, with the plan to return to work only after our kids were grown up. Kathy did get a part-time job during the school years and worked for about three years. Kathy became a Crossing Guard doing traffic before and after school on Byrne Road. This gave her a little spending money and she also added to our vacation fund. Kathy enjoyed the trips out west and being able to visit friends. Her plan was for us to retire in southern California. During the trips, the one place that had to be visited was Las Vegas as the gambling bug had bitten her. I can only blame myself, as I am the one, who introduced Kathy (and now Barb) to gambling.

As you can imagine, the second section of this book would be totally different, had life not thrown such a terrible curve at me. The book would still be written but from southern California and Kathy would be my typist. Life changes in an instant but anyone who knows what I am saying, also know that you must keep going and make a new way. The love and memories stay with you and you can be thankful for what time you have with a loved one. Back to thoughts and incidents during the 31 years as a police officer.

HOW SURPRISING AN ARREST CAN BE:

I was working fill in onWagon-4 patrol with Officer Bose. We were dispatched to Monroe and Superior on a Man-Down. We arrived and observed a male, flat on his back, in the roadway. Upon approaching him, we smelled the strong odor of intoxicants. We attempted to wake him and when unable to do so, we picked him up and put in the back of the wagon. Told dispatch we were going to Mercy Hospital to be treated. In those days we were able to call and book a subject, which we did. The hospital took charge and another crew was sent to transport to the jail. We left and a short time later dispatch called us to let us know our arrestee had “ESCAPED”.

We drove to the area and started searching. Another crew was able to locate him and took him to jail. We thought the matter was ended but dispatch called and told us to report to the building and see the Captain. When we went in the office, we found the “drunk”, and our Captain. Our Captain asked, “Do you know who this man is?” We explained that we had obtained his name from his wallet. The Captain then told us that the man was the

ASSISTANT WARDEN AT A PRISON IN MICHIGAN. "Oh boy! There goes my career!!"

The Captain asked us what happened and we told him about the man's condition and that he had escaped from the hospital. The Captain turned to drunk and said, "OK book him" and this was another case that we never went to court on….

In law enforcement it is the law not who you are – rich, poor, famous, star, average worker, criminal – YOU DO THE CRIME – YOU DO THE TIME. But, of course, we all see it happen too often – the powerful gets the slap on the hand while the poor person gets jail.

Just writing this book brought back so many memories of the "homes" we went into and the conditions people live in. On many occasions the odor coming from a residence was so overwhelming you asked to talk with the people outside. Wintertime was worse because the heat was turned on HIGH… Human and animal waste on the floors, urine stained mattresses where children slept. Live, and dead cockroaches, were found in every part of the residence. Plates, with whatever on it, which had decayed to an unrecognizable state. Tubs, toilets and sinks so filthy you would not let a dog be around, much less children, and the resident or woman telling you, "oh, I haven't been able to clean this week, I had a cold." As a cop you just stand there in amazement, also "keeping the feet moving" and "never sitting down".

Part of the enjoyment of a long career is watching "how things change" especially in the area of technology and equipment. When I started the cars only had the single "gumball" light on the top but through the years we transitioned to variations of the "light bar". The radios were the same. Of course, way before me – all officers had were phones to contact the building. Radio cars were invented but foot patrol still only had the call boxes. The portable radio was invented and towards the end the "collar mike" was developed. Officer safety and ease of use helps to bring about new fangled gadgets. From the nightstick and revolver, to the Asp and Capstun, and now that I am retired they developed the Taser. Now that would have come in handy those nights I fought on dance and bar room floors.

THE FIRING RANGE:

In the beginning, oh so many, many years ago – Toledo Police had a world class firing range. Officers from throughout the country and world would come for competitions. They had moving targets and courses like you see in Dirty Harry movies. What happened? Well as you all know, a city can do things that are totally stupid. Our range became the City Golf Course and where did the officers go to qualify…the area just beside the City Dump. We did for a while get to use the FBI's in-door range however after a period of time, several folks were found to have lead poisoning as the exhaust system was outdated. The department was able, towards our last few years on the department, to build a wonderful, in-door range. It also had space for classrooms and it became our "south substation". From good, to bad, to good…. that is how it goes many times. The dump location was not too bad when it was not hot and the smell overwhelming. There was a small range house and we used it to do entry training and actually, we had a range house "snake". He lived there year-round and more than likely kept the vermin count low.

ABORTION CLINICS:

This is not a statement as to my personal feelings about abortion. As a police officer you enforce the law – not your personal agenda. Toledo went through several years of situations involving the clinics and the protestors. I personally was involved over that period of time with a minimum of 6 or 7 demonstrations. We had one clinic on Monroe and another on Superior.

As I was currently in the Traffic Section, I was utilized as a "picture taker" with the Polaroid. Once I arrived at the demonstration, I would take several pictures of each person arrested along with the arresting officer. This was done because of the amount of arrests and keeping track of each officer's arrest. It helped when the cases came to court. Remember people can start to look alike and cases can take months to get to court, an officer needs something to make sure the memory is correct.

One memorable incident happened on Monroe and it involved several protestors had placed cement forms on their feet with a chain wrapped around the cement, foot and pole. The cement was molded to the foot. The officers were able to obtain bolt cutters and the folks were cut free and then transported – cement and all.

Another comical one was at the Superior Clinic. A very heavy set man (and for all you older TPD readers – we know he is "Pear Shape") had chained himself around his neck to a bar on the outside of the clinic window. Of course, Pear Shape threw away the key to the lock. Did I mention that this was on a very "hot" Toledo summer afternoon? After a period of time the "chained man" was asking for water and we helped him – which was our duty. We helped him a lot – he kept asking for water and we felt it our duty to provide assistance. The employees at the clinic also gave him water when he asked –

however they were on the roof and you can imagine how the water was delivered!

He spent quite a bit of time chained as it was taking time for the wagons to transport the various arrests and get back to the demonstration. He started asking to be "cut loose" as it seems all the water had done its work and he needed to go to the bathroom. After a period of pleading, he was cut free and, after a photograph, was transported to the jail. Due to the circumstances, he had to wait till he got booked in as there were no toilets available outside the clinic.

As a final note, the clinics started experiences more violence than "demonstrations" and this is when your personal beliefs need to be put away and you do your job. There were several arsons and fire bombings and interestingly, a security video showed a very distinct dark shape in the form of a pear……………. What may be somewhat righteous, civil expression turns to deadly, ugly violence and possible death to innocent bystanders.

PRESENT TIME

May 1994, after Barb retired from TPD with 21 1/2 years, we moved to Brookings, Oregon, which sits on the coast. It is located 6 miles above the California border. I had originally told Barb that I was just going to sit and enjoy retirement. No that did not happen and should never happen to any of you who plan retirement. You sit back and you die. We saw so many officers retire and within less than a couple years they passed away. When you have lived on "adrenalin" so long, you cannot just stop. You must have plans for another career, activity, anything to make the "life after law enforcement".

I started driving part-time for Dial-A-Ride (driving fellow seniors) and teaching AARP Drivers Safety Program. Barb, then a Brookings Police office, enlisted me into being McGruff, the Crime Dog. In 1998, after hearing comments about children not crossing streets correctly and not wearing helmets, I went back to Toledo and contacted the officers assigned to SAFETY CITY. TPD has run the program for decades and I thought it was a good idea for Brookings. With the help of the city, VIPS (Volunteers in Police Service) and community donations, Brookings Safety City started. This will be our 12th year running the program. The local grade school gives us a classroom and has allowed us to paint the "streets on the playground". We take 5 year old children (entering kindergarten) for a week, 2 1/2 hours daily, and instruct them in every possible "safety" area we can –

forest, water, 9-1-1, cops, good touch/bad touch, fire, animal, riding school buses and traffic/pedestrian safety. Monday to Friday they have class and then Saturday they graduate. We conduct (3) one-week programs during the summer. I guess 'ole traffic cops can learn new tricks.

LaVergne, TN USA
14 September 2010
197036LV00004B/71/P